Contents

- 3 R&A Championship Committee
- 5 Welcome: Chairman of Carnoustie Golf Links Management Committee
- 6 Spectator Facilities
- 10 Review of the 1998 Open Championship
  by Art Spander
- 20 "New boys, stand up and be strong" – Open Debutants
  by Mark Garrod
- 36 A Unique Appeal – Official Open Golf merchandise
  by Karen Giles
- 46 Classics at Carnoustie
  by Ian Wood
- 54 Carnoustie – A hole-by-hole guide
  by Keith Mackie
- 94 Players from countries with no tradition of championship golf
  by Renton Laidlaw
- 102
- 114 The Walker Cup returns to Scotland
  by Scott Crockett
- 120 The other fairways of the Open Championship
  by George Makey
- 127 Prize Fund
- 129 Players Exempt from Qualification
- 130 Exemption Qualifications
- 133 Past Winners
- 134 Final Scores in 1998
- 138 Course Map
- 140 Open Championship Statistics
- 142 Tented Village
- 146 Open Golf Show
- 151 Future Venues

The Royal and Ancient Golf Club of St. Andrews

128TH OPEN GOLF CHAMPIONSHIP

1999 Championship Committee

Chairman
H. M. Campbell

Deputy Chairman
R. M. Burns

Committee

P. E. Bechmann	N. M. Stephens
J. J. N. Caplan	J. M. Kippax
M. S. R. Lunt	M. C. Grint
R. D. Muckart	P. D. Montgomery
A. J. N. Loudon	M. C. Tate

J. L. S. Pasquill

Additional Member
M. N. Doyle, *Council of National Golf Unions*

Secretary
Sir Michael Bonallack, O.B.E.

Championship Secretary
D. Hill

Assistant Secretary (Championships)
D. R. Weir

Assistant Secretary (Championships)
A. E. Farquhar

Carnoustie *Country*

WALKING ON WATER

Whoever wins the Open at Carnoustie this year will be regarded by many as being able to walk on water. Should that be possible, he need only walk 12 miles across the Tay Estuary to defend his title at St. Andrews in 12 months.

If you would like to follow in his footsteps (on land!) and play the Championship Course or any of the other 21 notable courses in Carnoustie Country, dial **01241 417552** and ask for a Guide to Carnoustie Country outlining course details, accommodation and other tourist information.

Relax and catch the sweet spot!

A Message of Welcome from the Chairman of Carnoustie Golf Links Management Committee

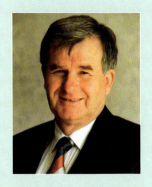

It is with great pleasure that I take this opportunity to welcome all competitors, spectators, officials and everyone else who is connected with the 128th Open Championship to Carnoustie. Everyone here is extremely proud that the Championship is returning again after a gap of 24 years and I am sure that a Champion worthy of standing alongside the five previous winners at Carnoustie will receive the Claret Jug at the culmination of this year's event.

Certain changes have taken place to the course over the intervening years all with a view to retaining it as a truly great test of golf. The field which will assemble will demonstrate their undoubted skills throughout the week and they will certainly engender further interest in this magnificent game.

Angus McKay

The Carnoustie Golf Links Open Championship Committee

A. McKay *(Chairman)*

B. Ogilvie *(Chief Marshal)*
W.D. Ramsay *(Deputy Chief Marshal)*
M.C. Richardson *(Staff Recruitment)*
P.J. Robb *(Chief Recorder)*
J. Clark *(Chief Scorer)*
E.J.C. Smith *(Secretary)*

H. Gibson *(Greens Convenor)*
J.S. Philp *(Links Superintendent)*
C.A. Fenton *(Car Parking)*
G. Wilson *(Environment/Litter)*
C. Healey *(Deputy Chief Scorer)*
J.M. Martin *(Executive Secretary)*

Spectator Facilities

SCORING INFORMATION
A comprehensive information system is operated to keep spectators in touch with the play around the course.

HOLE APPROACH BOARDS
Located at most greens and show the current score in terms of par, for the round being played and cumulative for the Championship, for each player approaching that particular green.

LEADER BOARDS
Show the current leaders in the Championship based on the cumulative scores in terms of par for the holes played by each player and are situated adjacent to and are clearly visible from most spectating stands. There will also be leader boards sited in the Tented Village.

MAIN SCOREBOARDS
The hole-by-hole board is sited within the Tented Village. The other board showing completed scores for the round is to the right of the 7th fairway.

CATERING, TOILETS AND FIRST AID
Public catering facilities are available in the Tented Village and at other points on the course. Toilets and first aid points are to be found within the Tented Village and also on the course.

SPECTATOR MOVEMENT
Spectators will find that they can move freely to all parts of the course. To assist spectator movement there are controlled crossings over fairways.

There are certain areas on the course to which there will be no access, but this is for reasons of the unsuitability of the ground or because these areas are 'in play'.

A 'Red Route' has been shown clearly on the map on pages 138 and 139 in the Programme. This route has been designed for the benefit of spectators who may wish to follow a particular game for a complete round from the 1st tee to the 18th green. The route will enable spectators to move freely and quickly to vantage points where they may obtain the best possible view of the play at each hole. The signposts indicating this route will be red with white lettering.

CAMERAS
Spectators are not allowed to bring cameras on to the course on Championship days. They will however be able to borrow a Nikon camera on the Practice Ground throughout the Championship week and take shots of the players practising.

In conjunction with Nikon U.K. Limited, the Championship Committee of the Royal and Ancient Golf Club are delighted to be able to provide this facility for spectators at the Practice Ground area.

A Nikon camera loaded with a 12 exposure print film will be provided for use by spectators, and a member of Nikon's staff will be on hand to offer assistance and advice.

SPECTATOR INFORMATION
By observing the following rules everyone will have an opportunity to see the play in comfort and the players will enjoy the best playing conditions.

(a) Please obey the marshals, keep behind ropes and barriers and use the designated crossing points.
(b) Please display your admission ticket at all times.
(c) Some spectator stands are located close to greens. Movement in the stands may distract players, so please do not move in or out of the stands while putting is in progress.
(d) Carnoustie is very attractive. Please help to keep it so by depositing any litter or rubbish in the containers provided.
(e) No cameras may be taken on the course from Thursday 15th–Sunday 18th July.
(f) Step ladders are not permitted within the paygates and should not be brought to the course.
(g) Mobile phones can disrupt the competitors during play and should not be brought to the course.
(h) No dogs are allowed on the course.

OPEN CHAMPIONSHIP WEBSITE

For the fastest and most accurate scoring service available on the Internet and all the latest tournament news, visit the official Open Championship website at www.opengolf.com. The site contains details about the players, the course and the history of the Championship as well as useful information for spectators. Visitors can also purchase official Open Championship merchandise directly from the website.

FACILITIES FOR THE DISABLED

The Royal and Ancient Golf Club are happy once again to announce the following facilities for disabled persons at this year's Open Championship:
Special car parking.
Space for wheelchairs around the 18th green.
A specially built toilet unit—located close by the 18th green.

DAILY STARTING TIMES

	First tee-off	Last tee-off
Thursday 15th July	7.15a.m.	3.45p.m.
Friday 16th July	7.15a.m.	3.45p.m.
Saturday 17th July	8.55a.m.(approx.)	3.15p.m.
Sunday 18th July	8.25a.m.(approx.)	2.45p.m.

VIEWING SCREEN

A large Diamond Vision Screen, located in the Tented Village, will show live BBC TV coverage of the Championship.

THANK YOU

The Royal & Ancient Golf Club of St Andrews thank all volunteers at this year's Open for their efforts in ensuring the success of the Championship.

RADIO COMMENTARY
BBC RADIO 5 LIVE
909 & 693 MW

There will be regular reports on the build-up to the Championship from Monday July 12th on BBC Radio 5–Live (909/693MW) with sports bulletins every half-hour, 24 hours a day.
Once the Championship begins…
Thursday 15th July:
Reports on BBC Radio 5–Live every 15 mins from 7.00am –1.30pm. Commentary on the day's play in a special golf programme between 1.00pm and 8.00pm.
Friday 16th July:
Reports on BBC Radio 5–Live every 15 mins from 7.00am –1.30pm. Commentary on the day's play in a special golf programme between 1.00pm and 8.00pm.
Saturday 17th July:
Reports on BBC Radio 5–Live every 15 mins 7.00am–1.30pm.
1.00pm–8.00pm: live coverage of the day's play.
Sunday 18th July:
Reports on BBC Radio 5–Live every 15 mins from 7.00am –1.30pm. Commentary on the climax of the Championship between 1.00pm and 7.00pm.

CHILDREN 1st (Royal Society for Prevention of Cruelty to Children) is delighted to have been nominated as the official Charity for the 1999 Open Championship at Carnoustie. CHILDREN 1st is Scotland's own child-care agency, and is dedicated to protecting Scotland's children suffering from abuse and neglect, and ensuring parents have the essential support to provide their children with a brighter future. 90% of our income comes from voluntary sources and stays in Scotland to support Scotland's children and families.

Tiger Woods

UNITED STATES

BORN
30th December 1975, Cypress, California

MAJORS
US Masters 1997

CARNOUSTIE IS THE PLACE OF LEGENDS: ARMOUR, COTTON, HOGAN, PLAYER, WATSON.

AND ROLEX.

After an absence of nearly a quarter of a century, the British Open returns to Carnoustie. As past Open champions will testify, it has taken the finest players of their generation to master these stern and unforgiving windswept Scottish links. And to witness the new generation of players setting off in hope, and returning perhaps in triumph, stands the world's largest Rolex. On such a course where only the strongest mettle prevails, is it any wonder that Rolex – the chosen timepiece of generations of golfing legends – is the official timekeeper?

ROLEX
of Geneva

ROLEX. OFFICIAL TIMEKEEPER TO THE 1999 BRITISH OPEN GOLF CHAMPIONSHIP.

"I think I'm a very nice player, a good player, but I don't classify myself as great."

Mark O'Meara

Mark O'Meara and Nick Faldo, Royal Birkdale 1998

H e had embraced the silver claret jug before, when it was under the temporary control of a man who sadly would lose control of so much more.

Ian Baker-Finch is one of Mark O'Meara's friends and had been one of his neighbours in Florida. And so O'Meara would hoist the Open trophy and sip champagne after being invited to drop by and share in the joy of Baker-Finch's 1991 triumph at Royal Birkdale.

Surely there was something mystical about it all, something beyond our comprehension if not beyond O'Meara's grasp.

Because on the very same links land, the

> Art Spander, one of America's leading sports writers, recalls the high and low points of the 1998 Open

raggedy, wind-swept, enticing dunes of Royal Birkdale, O'Meara would again hold the claret jug. But now it was his, not anyone else's.

Now Mark O'Meara was the Open champion, paying homage to Baker-Finch whose game has disintegrated.

And there was O'Meara insisting he had no idea how a professional career that went 17 years without one major championship wouldn't go four more months without a second.

That he had no idea how, at 41 years six months and six days, Mark O'Meara would become the oldest player ever to take two majors in a calendar year.

What a great climax to a great Open, being played for the 127th time and carrying so much history and tradition. What a remarkable final day of rain and wind and emotion. And irony.

O'Meara had tied for first with Brian Watts, an American who had been playing in Japan. Each had shot 280, which was even par, and wasn't that interesting? Because it was even par which gave Lee Janzen the U.S. Open a month earlier at San Francisco's Olympic Club.

We knew O'Meara. Not only because in April he had slipped on the green jacket at Augusta. After all, he had been tied with Baker-Finch for the lead after three rounds of the 1991 Open. And he had also been his playing partner on the final day when Baker-Finch shot 66 for first and O'Meara 69 to tie for third.

So we knew O'Meara, and O'Meara knew Birkdale, not only having the excellent Open seven years earlier despite an ailing back but winning the Lawrence Batley Classic there in 1987.

Few, however, knew Watts.

"I had dinner at a Chinese restaurant in Southport on Saturday night," he mused. "I don't think anybody recognized me. I don't think anybody knew who I was. And I was leading the tournament."

Indeed, an impressive 73 during a weather-battered third round in which Phil Mickelson shot 85 and defending champ Justin Leonard 82, Watts was, at 210, in front by two strokes over Jesper Parnevik, Jim Furyk and O'Meara.

But coming down to the 72nd hole, with Birkdale's white-washed, ship's cabin of a clubhouse hard behind the green, Watts was tied with O'Meara, who was already finished.

And when Watts hit his approach shot onto the back downslope of a bunker, it seemed he also might be finished.

Watts, however, responded with the most memorable shot of the Open, a shot reminiscent

Brian Watts tees off during the play-off

of Costantino Rocca's mammoth putt through the Valley of Sin to tie John Daly at St. Andrews in '95.

With his right foot outside the trap and his left foot in the sand, Watts, maybe 35 yards from the hole, blasted to within inches to save par. That he couldn't save a championship in no way diminished his performance.

Watts and O'Meara went into the unique play-off the Open utilises, four holes, right now. It's long enough to be fair, so one lucky shot won't determine the champion of the oldest tournament in the world. Yet unlike the 18-hole Monday play-off to which the U.S. Open clings, it doesn't lose any of the immediacy or intensity.

O'Meara birdied the first play-off hole, the par-five 15th, and he would never trail. He finished one-under, while Watts came in at one over.

For O'Meara, it was a week of guts and putts. For the Open it was a week of more subplots than an Agatha Christie novel, a week that began with people losing balls in the weeds during practice rounds and ended with some of the players having lost their temper.

The drama began ever before the

Brian Watts

competition. Lee Janzen came off the course on Tuesday like someone seeking a Southport in a storm. The wind had gusted to 40 miles an hour, and the man who a month earlier won the other Open was frustrated. And frosted.

"I told my caddie I should try to hit the ball into the rough," Janzen said, "and then just play wedge shots up to the green. He wasn't sure I was serious."

Anyone in the field at Birkdale, with its moonscape views, its fairways twisting like a maze through the bushes and high rough, had to be serious.

The sun came out and the wind eased for day one, and four of the top five on the leaderboard were from the United States, with the fifth, Nick Price, basically also from the U.S. even though he carries a passport from Zimbabwe.

There was a time when Americans couldn't do anything in Great Britain except turn in their VAT receipts at customs. But after 18 holes, Tiger Woods and John Huston were at five-under par 65, while tied for third were Fred Couples, Loren Roberts and Mr. Price.

Watts had everyone asking "Who's he?" after the second round when Brian shot a 69 to move in front with a three-under

Justin Rose

par 137. Price and Woods would be tied for second at 138 with another golfer who not only made headlines but also a bit of history.

Justin Rose, a 17-year-old from Hook in Hampshire, hadn't been exempt for the 156 man field, even though a GB&I Walker Cup team member. His opening round 72 was lost among the scores. But on Friday, Justin had low round of the day, a 66, in the sort of weather for which Opens are infamous and which caused the average score to reach 74.76.

With the rest of Britain's stars, Colin Montgomerie, Nick Faldo and Lee Westwood, as one newspaper phrased it, "playing like amateurs," it was the amateur who became the star. Fans put roses in their caps and shouted Justin's name from packed galleries.

Day three, the shouting was done by the entrants. The weather was, well, brutal. Royal Birkdale is fortunate it wasn't blown back to the 19th Century.

Mickelson shot his 85, Leonard and Price 82s, Janzen 80 and Tiger Woods 77. "It's not a fair test of golf," whined Woosnam, who had a decent 76. "They set the course up for a 10 to 15-mile an hour wind, but it was blowing 30. That's too tough."

Leonard could only offer gallows humor. "Now," he said after finishing early, "I'm going back to watch the afternoon's play on TV and laugh at the other guys playing."

There was no laughter from, or at, O'Meara. There might have been some sighs.

On the killer sixth hole, the 480-yard par-four disguised as a par-five, on which there were only 16 birdies in 472 attempts during the entire championship, O'Meara lost his approach in the junk.

After a three to four-minute search failed to turn up the ball, he began to walk back to the spot where he had hit when suddenly a spectator found the ball and put it in his pocket.

"There was a lot of miscommunication," said O'Meara. "The USGA was on the radio. The R&A was on the radio. It was like Watergate. Nobody would make the call." Finally, he was

Tiger Woods

allowed a free drop and made bogey.

On Sunday, O'Meara was as far back of Watts as three strokes after seven holes. But birdies at 11 and 12 gave him a one-shot edge. Each was at one-over through 16 and each birdied 17 to get to even, where they would finish.

Tiger shot 66 to miss the play-off by a shot, while Rose would sink a 45-yard wedge shot on 18 for a birdie that left him tied for fourth, the best finish in the Open by an amateur since Frank Stranahan, at Carnoustie, in 1953.

What would turn out to be Rose's final shot as an amateur caused the home crowd to erupt over the home boy. When the cheers finally ebbed, Sir Michael Bonallack, Secretary of the Royal & Ancient shook his head and insisted, "That was the loudest roar I have ever heard on a golf course."

When O'Meara spoke at the ceremonies after the round, he wasn't loud, only humble.

Asked if wins in two majors gave him a place in history, O'Meara answered, "No.

"I think I'm a very nice player, a good player, but I don't classify myself as great. Jack Nicklaus, Byron Nelson, Ben Hogan, Sam Snead, Arnold Palmer, those are great golfers."

O'Meara is a persistent golfer. He's also a superb putter. So many players hate being identified like that, as if putting is a stigma, something less than, say, a beautiful swing.

"But if they want to say that about me, fine," contended O'Meara. "Putting is half the game, isn't it?

Two years ago, in a magazine article, O'Meara was labelled, "King of the B's," as in "B" or second-grade movies. He won numerous tournaments, including the Crosby/AT&T five times. But he had never won a major.

Then in 1998 he wins two, knocking in a putt at the 72nd hole at Augusta for the first, needing a play-off at Royal Birkdale for the second. "I don't know why I've done it now," said O'Meara. "Maybe it's maturity. I know I will savour this victory as much, if not more, than what happened this year at Augusta. This is a special championship."

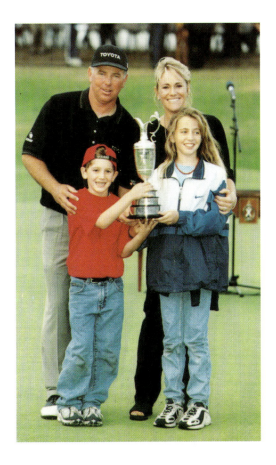

A sense of ACHIEVEMENT

It's what we feel on the completion of every CALA home. It's what you feel when you live in one.

Developments at: Abbot's Field, *Paisley* • Balmossie Mill, *Broughty Ferry, Dundee* • The Inveresk Estate, *East Lothian* • Kings Ridings, *Strathaven* • Meadowlands, *Westhill, Aberdeen* • Queen's View, *Aberdeen* • Regency Court, *Aberdeen* • Shanter's Wynd, *Cambusdoon, Alloway* • Stewart's Crest, *Bishopton* • Vernonholme Estate, *Dundee* • Victoria Court, *Scotstoun*

Coming Soon: *Developments in Aberdeen, Bridge of Allan, Bearsden, Dunblane, Dunfermline, Edinburgh, Haddington, Helensburgh, Gourock and West Linton*

For further details of CALA developments please telephone: 01324 638889

www.pwave.co.uk/pwave/cala

CALA HOMES

Darren Clarke

GREAT BRITAIN

BORN
14TH AUGUST 1968, DUNGANNON, NORTHERN IRELAND

Thumbs-up from a high flyer

Colin Montgomerie - In the cockpit of a Eurofighter Typhoon.

Thanks to everyone for making 1999's British Aerospace National Golf Week such a success. The event was staged throughout the UK and Ireland and thousands of free golf lessons were given to newcomers of all ages by PGA Professionals.

This is just one of the many examples of our ability to develop meaningful partnerships throughout the world, with governments, industry and the community. It is in this spirit of partnership that we drive forward with the world's best to produce outstanding aerospace and defence programmes.

We look forward to continuing our relationship with the PGA, Sportsmatch and the sport of golf in the coming years.

www.bae.co.uk

Ernie Els

SOUTH AFRICA

BORN
17TH OCTOBER 1969, JOHANNESBURG, SOUTH AFRICA

MAJORS
US OPEN 1994, 97

"New boys, stand up and be strong."

Ben Hogan, during the 1953 Championship

A question for you. Who were the last three players to win the Open on their first appearance in the Championship? Sorry, no prizes. But just be grateful that I did not ask the same question of the United States Open. No debutant has triumphed there since amateur Francis Ouimet way back in 1913.

Take a bow then if you answered Tom Watson (1975), Tony Lema (1964) and Ben Hogan (1953). And what else did Watson's and Hogan's victories have in common? They both came at Carnoustie. The wins were achieved by different means. Hogan, four years on from the car crash which nearly killed him and with the Masters

> Mark Garrod,
> Golf Correspondent for PA Sport,
> looks at the Open debutants –
> winners and nearly men.

and US Open of that season already in the bag, arrived a week early, both to accustom himself to the smaller British ball and also to learn what he could about links golf before the event began.

What most dismayed him on his arrival was the length of the grass on the greens. He even offered to have a lawnmower flown over. But it was not necessary - one got the feeling that if he had been asked to putt over mushy peas and Yorkshire pudding he would have learned the art. He was in a league of his own and, lowering his score in each round, took his ninth major title by four strokes. Only a clash of dates with the USPGA Championship (match play in those days) prevented him trying for an unprecedented "Grand Slam" of all four majors in one year.

Watson's approach, on the other hand, was

Tony Lema, Champion at St. Andrews in 1964

described by Peter Alliss as "a disgracefully planned campaign." He had hardly played a hole prior to the first round, leaving it to British caddie Alfie Fyles to point him the way and hand him the clubs. But it worked – Watson blew away his reputation as a poor finisher by making a 15-foot closing putt for a play-off with Australian Jack Newton and won the following day.

Hogan never returned. Watson did, of course. By 1983 he had lifted the famous claret jug four more times and, but for Severiano Ballesteros' dramatic finish in 1984, he might have equalled Harry Vardon's record six titles.

The players making their debuts this time will be filled with thoughts of what might be. However they have qualified for the championship - be it amateurs like new British Champion Graeme Storm and European Champion Paddy Gribben, from Northern Ireland, and professionals like Jarrod Moseley, whose shock victory in the Heineken Classic in Australia in January opened all sorts of doors - they know they are capable of great golf under pressure. They have all done it; they just have not done it in the Open before.

Remember Justin Rose 12 months ago. How could we forget? At just 17 he came through the final qualifying competition on the Sunday and Monday of Open week to earn the right to line up with the stars at Royal Birkdale.

That was enough to make it a memorable experience, but what followed was the stuff of dreams. Rose's Friday 66 was better than any of the world's biggest names could manage. It lifted him into joint second place with Tiger Woods and Nick Price and when he pitched in from 45

Jack Newton with Open Champion, Tom Watson at Carnoustie in 1975

yards for an 18th hole birdie two days later, his joint fourth spot represented the best by an amateur in the Open for 45 years - since American Frank Stranahan was joint runner-up behind Hogan - and the first top 10 finish by an amateur in any major for 27 years.

He had been followed by the Duke of York, groups of teenage girls squealed (they were dubbed "Rosettes") and he had become a household name. That is what the Open can do for you.

To be able to seize the moment is the thing. Colin Montgomerie came up with a little ditty at Wentworth in May when called upon to receive the Vardon Trophy as Europe's leading money-winner for a record sixth successive time.

"If not me, who? If not now, when?" he recited.

It looked like a mantra adopted by Jose Maria Olazabal for his second Masters victory just a month earlier. If anything demonstrated the power of the mind that did. Olazabal appeared to will himself out of whatever predicament he placed himself in as he marched - something he could not do three years ago - to glory.

So new boys, stand up and be strong. Did John Daly flinch for a moment when called into his USPGA debut in 1991 after originally being the ninth reserve? Did his great friend Fuzzy Zoeller crack at the thought of winning the Masters at the first attempt in 1979?

Choose your method - the Hogan Way if you believe knowledge is power, the Watson Way if you reckon the less you know the less you have to be frightened of - and go do it.

Colin Montgomerie

The 1998 European Amateur Individual Champion, Paddy Gribben

BA popular person.

Fly Club World and take a friend free the next time you travel.

Fly Concorde, First or Club World before 31st July and, the next time you travel you can take anyone free, to any of our destinations around the world in any class. Any service charges or passenger taxes will still apply. To see how easy it is yourself, call 0345 114 116, visit www.britishairways.com, contact your travel agent or British Airways Travel Shop now.

BRITISH AIRWAYS
The world's favourite airline

Passenger taxes, fees and charges apply and will be chargeable to and payable by each passenger. To qualify you must be UK resident, enrolled in our Executive Club and fly Concorde, First or Club World (excluding some discount, leisure and promotional fares) between 4th May and 31st July 1999. Free companion flights must be from the UK and taken by 30th September 1999. Flights are subject to capacity control and availability. Other terms and conditions apply. For more information or to join the Executive Club call 0345 114 116.

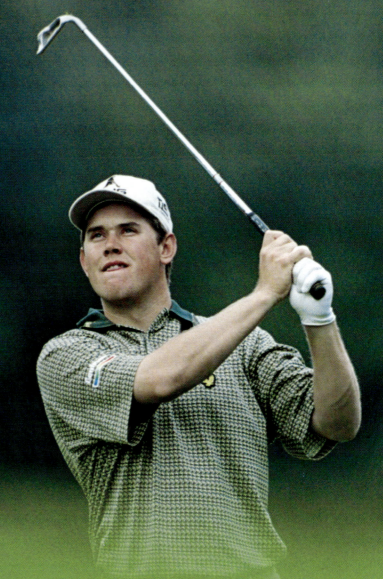

Lee Westwood

GREAT BRITAIN

BORN
24TH APRIL 1973, WORKSOP, ENGLAND

Vijay Singh

FIJI

BORN
22nd February 1963, Lautoka, Fiji

MAJORS
USPGA 1998

Carnoustie.
One of the most challenging golf courses in the world.

Make sure you give it your best shot.

Callaway GOLF
How Golf Should Feel

ODYSSEY
Number one putter in golf

Callaway®, How Golf Should Feel®, Hawk Eye®, Steelhea
X-12™, Dual Force®, Rossie™, Odyssey® and Number
Putter in Golf™ are trademarks of Callaway Golf Compa

Colin Montgomerie

GREAT BRITAIN

BORN
23RD JUNE 1963, GLASGOW, SCOTLAND

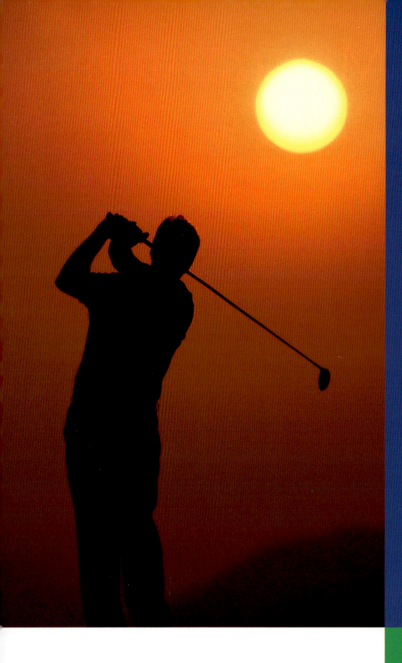

Royal & SunAlliance

Best UK Investment Management Group

STANDARD & POOR'S Micropal AWARDS — 1997 and 1998

The Open Champion of investment...

...and sponsor of the Rules of Golf since 1908

Royal & Sun Alliance Investment Management Limited is regulated by IMRO. Registered in England, No 2219464. Registered Office: St. Mark's Court, Chart Way, Horsham, West Sussex, RH12 1XL.

Joe Ozaki

JAPAN

BORN
18TH MAY 1956, TOKUSHIMA, JAPAN

LEE JANZEN

UNITED STATES

BORN
28TH AUGUST 1964, AUSTIN, MINNESOTA

MAJORS
US OPEN 1993, 98

train fare from Edinburgh: £27

5 nights in Carnoustie: £350

tickets to all 4 rounds of the Open Championship: £100

souvenir programme: £5

not watching it on TV: priceless

there are some things money can't buy.
for everything else there's MasterCard.

Official Card of the 128th Open Championship and friend to golfers everywhere.

Severiano Ballesteros

SPAIN

BORN
9th April 1957, Pedrena, Spain

MAJORS
The Open 1979, 84, 88 • US Masters 1980, 83

CARNOUSTIE

A UNIQUE APPEAL

If it's a Claret Jug bubble bath you're after, or an Old Course duvet cover with matching lamp shade and curtains, I'm afraid you've had it. There's not a 'Monty is Ace' tee-shirt in sight and nor, for that matter, any fluffy Faldos, engraved tea strainers or embossed chamois leathers. Those of a less-discerning palate be warned. The stands boasting the official merchandise of this year's Open Championship are decidedly upmarket, very tasteful and of top-notch quality. The emphasis is on the exclusive.

Karen Giles examines the story behind the unique appeal of the Open Championship brand name

The Open has come a long way since visitors to the championship departed the course with nothing more significant than a programme and a wonky, cardboard periscope. Where once you would do well to purchase a polyester/cotton polo shirt without an outlandish collar in cobalt blue, today's carefully selected range of products, all branded with the official Open 'lozenge' logo, reflect modern day golf and its increasing popularity, whilst retaining a certain exclusivity.

Everyone, it seems, now wants a piece of the Open Championship. Be it a pillar-box red baseball cap or yellow lemon lambswool sweater, the demand for official products has developed into a profitable business. So much so that, next year, for the 2000 Open Championship at the Old Course, St Andrews, an exclusive range will be unveiled. Again the emphasis is on quality. From engraved buttons to embossed buckles, watch out for the Open's new navy and white collection.

It has the backing of the Royal & Ancient and is the brainchild of Mervyn Campbell, a Glasgow-based businessman. Head of Greenways Marketing International, Campbell's company is the official licensee of the Open logo. No-one other than Campbell can produce merchandise resplendent with the Claret Jug and the Open title. It is a contract he has fiercely protected since 1990, with hard work and enthusiasm ensuring an extension at least until Royal Lytham & St Annes in 2001.

Under Campbell's guidance, the sale of official merchandise is no longer low key and unco-ordinated. Four impressive stands will draw attention to new products at Carnoustie this year, two within the Golf

Show tent. The introduction of a mail order service and the use of the Internet to promote the range, will only improve a turnover that has already increased twenty-fold since Campbell's involvement. Next summer, the mouthwatering combination of St Andrews, the Open and the Millenium should force sales over the £1 million mark.

Across the Atlantic such a figure would be scoffed at. Sales at the US Open are believed to generate in excess of $7 million. Campbell, however, rejects the suggestion that the Open is heading in the same direction of hard sell and inflated prices. Although business has progressed "dramatically" over the years, the Open does not have the same selling potential as Stateside where ticket restrictions, amongst other things, encourage the extraordinary sale of commemorative gifts. And as Campbell wryly observed: "The Americans are just loopy about buying things."

Arms full of pinflags

Take for instance the armful of replica pin flags bought by Mark O'Meara as gifts at Royal Birkdale last year. "They are exceptionally popular," observed Campbell with a smile. "We introduced them two years ago at Troon and had no idea whether we had got the price right or whether the public would want to buy them. On the Tuesday, after just a day and a half of being on sale, I had to order the same again." They are now an established piece of merchandise, a replica of the 18th flag, nicely boxed and a bargain at £20! Just ask O'Meara.

Sixteen years of Open selling has taught Campbell a thing or two about golfing tastes and foibles. "The Japanese always buy in multiples of ten. The Americans are enthusiastic about everything. A few years ago I had a very well-to-do American lady enquiring about visors. She asked if they were bi-sexual. It was almost as funny as the guy who came to buy a flat cap so that he could imitate his hero Per-Ulrik Johansson. When handed one, he asked whether we had any that pointed the other way round."

Headwear is now Campbell's biggest individual seller and reflects perfectly the modernisation of the industry not to mention the shift in fashions. "When I first started out, we only sold visors and flat caps. Nowadays baseball caps are where its at. We sell anything between 5,000 and 10,000 caps per Open depending, of course, on the weather." Again the attention to detail is impressive. None of your plastic rubbish. Velcro or leather adjustable straps with buckles featuring the Claret Jug, thank you very much.

Remember to look out for the four R&A exclusive merchandise selling points; two in the tented village and two in the Open Golf Show.

No product escapes quality control. From autograph pen, affordable for the youngsters, to the top of the range knitwear, a lady's cotton v-neck sweater in cable knit at £69.50, every purchase is carefully vetted by the Royal & Ancient in the Autumn prior to sale. Campbell, who attends golf trade shows world-wide, has his finger on the pulse of fashion. The R&A, keen perhaps to relax their conservative, rather dated image, appear happy to accept his recommendations.

As demand for merchandise has increased, so has the R&A's involvement. Admits Campbell: "We work very closely together, deciding on the range, the colours, the styles and the prices. We are keen to ensure the pricing at the Open is as favourable to the public as any other golf tournament in the world, in fact probably even more favourable. For example the Ryder Cup is excessively high."

But times have changed. "In the old days, the smaller products were the ones that sold; ball markers and tees. Now people are looking for a shirt, sweater or an umbrella, all with the Open logo." Whatever they are after, Campbell's glamorous sales team are only too willing to search the four twenty foot containers required to house all stock on site. All of them attractive and recruited mainly from The Model Agency in Glasgow, Campbell's thirty-plus staff work long, arduous hours, manning 14 electronic sales tills.

"Although we open at 9am and finish at 6.30pm, when the Golf Show closes, outside, in the tented village, we continue until the last player comes off the course." And every sale is registered on the computer. "At any one time I know exactly how many red crew neck sweaters in medium we have available." Fridays are big. Campbell never orders extra stock on a Saturday night. Sales dip as the event reaches its climax. "The trick is not to be too greedy."

There are obvious logistical nightmares, headaches that can, and often do, turn into migraines. "We can't predict the weather. Last year it poured with rain and we ran out of umbrellas. But you should have seen the number of straw hats we had left over ! Where possible we have overnight back-up. I have a team of embroiderers who work through the night if I think we're getting a bit low on certain stock."

But there is no rhyme nor reason for it. "One year we will have a surplus of small sweaters, the next a shortage. We've done our best to try and guard against ending up with huge surpluses. Nowadays we don't date our knitwear. A nice sweater is a nice sweater. You don't need something that dates it. Most people are just happy to be at the Open."

Happy and hopefully delighted with this year's stylish Open accessory. It is Campbell's aim to please and it is his belief that a totally exclusive Open range is the way forward. "We hope that the products we sell are befitting the Open Championship. From September this year, we will be offering a limited range of exclusive goods, all identifying the Open 2000 at the Old Course. It promises to be a bit special."

Shopaholics, check out the web site: http://www.opengolf.com and have your credit cards ready…

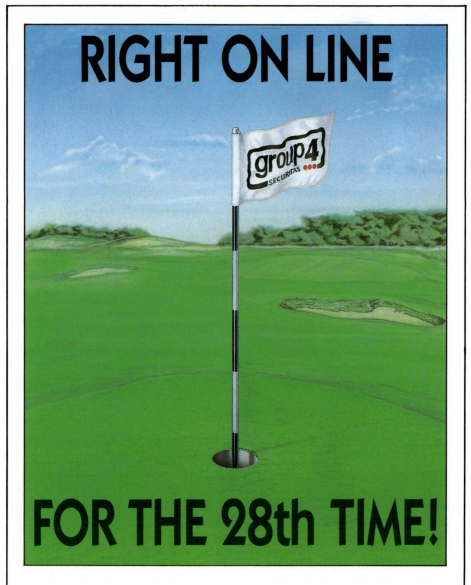

It's 28 years since Group 4 started providing annual security for the Open. And amazingly, 24 years since we were last here at this wonderfully tough course, when Tom Watson took possession of the Old Claret Jug. With so many brilliant contenders around, the '99 Championship is poised to be perhaps the most exciting ever. Be sure – Group 4 will help ensure that everyone enjoys this great golfing occasion to the full. Spectators, players and officials alike.

NEVER BELOW PAR
Group 4 Total Security Limited,
Farncombe House, Broadway, Worcs WR12 7LJ. Tel: 01386 858585

DAVID DUVAL

UNITED STATES

BORN
9TH NOVEMBER 1971, JACKSONVILLE, FLORIDA

FIRESOLE™ DRIVER

FIND THE YARDAGE TO YOUR SOUL

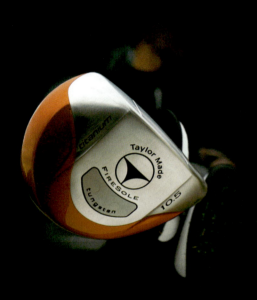

New FireSole Technology from Taylor Made will revolutionise your game. By using titanium, tungsten and steel in different combinations through the range of clubs, we've ensured that the right weight is in the right location for the right shot. That means every FireSole club is engineered to provide the precise combination of power and control to suit the shot you want to play.

The FireSole Driver is constructed around an explosive "power band." This holds energy and releases it directly to the ball on impact whilst a high density tungsten power plug positioned behind the sweet spot channels all available force where it is needed most, under and behind the ball. The solid, commanding impact you achieve with FireSole, delivers pure, precise and penetrating power.

FIND WEIGHT WHERE YOU NEED IT MOST

FIND YOUR GAME™

HAVE YOU TAKEN THE

For details of your nearest Demo Day phone: 0800 389 4292
www.taylormadegolf.com

Mark O'Meara

UNITED STATES

BORN
13th January 1957, Goldsboro, North Carolina

MAJORS
US Masters 1998 • The Open 1998

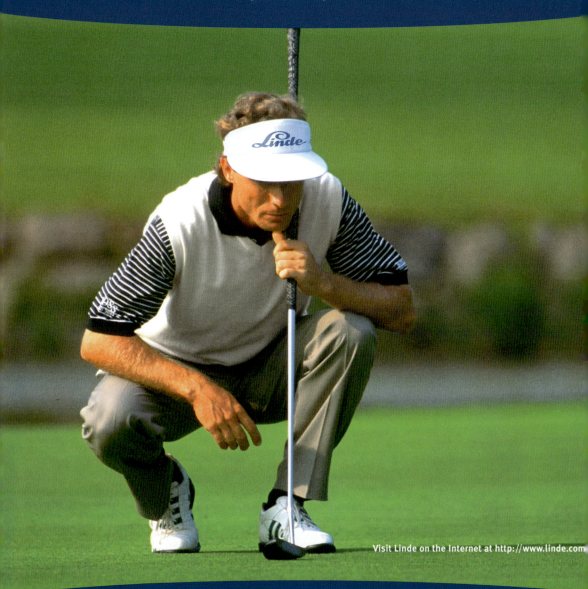

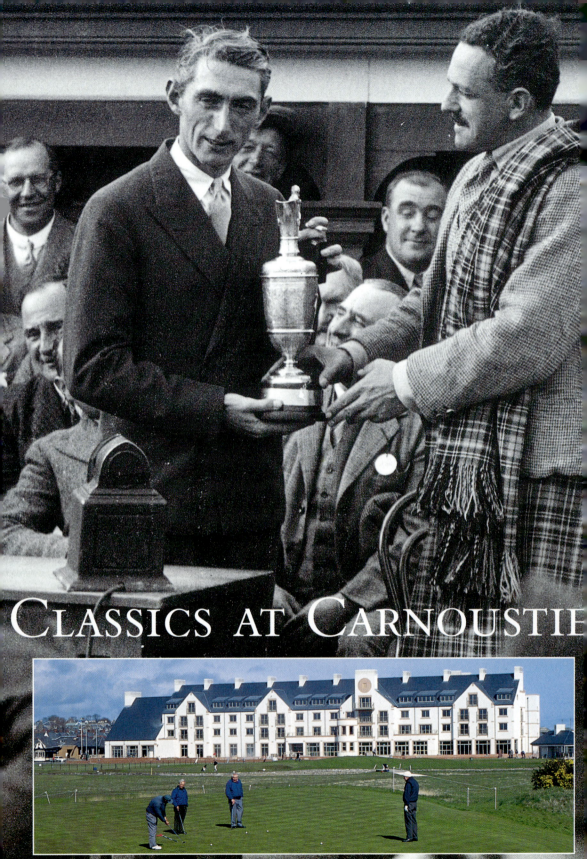

Classics at Carnoustie

Tommy Armour - 1931

Just as Augusta National, home of the US Masters, prompts words such as lush, manicured and breathtaking, so Carnoustie tends to be described as grim, gaunt and wild. That is as it should be, for traditional links are stern places and Carnoustie is a classic.

1931

When Tommy Armour, whose early game was honed on Edinburgh's Braid Hills, returned from America in 1931 to win the first Open to be held over the Angus course, his aggregate score of 296 was the highest winning total since Jim Barnes' 300 at Prestwick in 1925.

Ian Wood, columnist for The Scotsman, reviews the previous Open Championships held at Carnoustie

The last day of the 1931 championship – "the most pleasant of the week," it was reported – was played in a cold nor'-easter which took its toll of a field which included the Americans, Gene Sarazen, Macdonald Smith and Johnny Farrell, England's Henry Cotton and Percy Allis and, from Argentina, the man who was to run Armour closest, Jose Jurado, who went into the final round five shots ahead of the Scot.

Armour, who'd lost an eye during action in

the First World War, responded with a closing 71 which featured a mixture of splendid shot-making and resolute recovery play. He'd come to the championship having won the USPGA Championship the previous year and the US Open in 1927. Now, he needed to get down from a yard for his par at the last and was later to confess that it hadn't been easy.

"I took a new grip, holding the club as tightly as I could and with stiff wrists," he recalled. "From the instant the club left the ball on the backswing, I was blind and unconscious." While all that may sound chillingly familiar, it worked and Armour got home by a single stroke from Jurado.

1937

Henry Cotton in 1937

Henry Cotton had a miserable time of it in that Open, particularly around the greens, but he put things gloriously to rights in 1937 by overcoming the might of the US Ryder Cup side – Byron Nelson, Sam Snead, Horton Smith, Gene Sarazen, Ralph Guldahl *et al* – as well as weather conditions which threatened to render the course unplayable.

This time, Cotton's short game was inspired and, as his challengers wilted in the torrential rain – Reg Whitcombe, the eventual runner-up, caught the worst of it – he played the first six holes in two under par and, thus launched, held things together superbly for 71, a total of 290 and victory by two shots. It was the second of Cotton's three Open titles.

1953

Carnoustie's roll of honour is short but distinguished and the 1953 Championship added the name of Ben Hogan. The legendary American arrived as holder of the US Masters and US Open titles. The dominant figure in

world golf, he was expected to win and duly did, with rounds of 73, 71, 70 and 68.

The ruthless efficiency the British golfing public had heard about was there for all to see. Switching to the smaller British ball for greater distance, Hogan, who didn't like the cold and had his reservations about the greens, adjusted his swing so that he clipped his irons off the turf as opposed to taking divots.

Seldom can there have been such an inevitability about the outcome of an Open. It wasn't as if there was any lack of challengers. Bobby Locke, the defending champion, was there, as were the Argentinians, Roberto de Vicenzo and Tony Cerda, Scotland's Eric Brown, Wales' Dai Rees, England's Peter Alliss and the great American amateur, Frank Stranahan. Australia's Peter Thomson was present too, quietly readying himself for greatness.

Ben Hogan – 1953

Many had their moments in the last round – Stranahan single-putted the last six greens and posted a 3, 4, 3, 3 finish for a 69 – but mainly it was about Hogan. He missed the fifth green, but sank the chip for a birdie. A shot got away from him at the fourteenth after he'd birdied the short thirteenth. There was little more to it apart from perfection. Hogan won by four shots from Thomson, Rees, Cerda and Stranahan, with a total of 282.

1968

Things were tighter when Gary Player won his second championship in 1968. Typically, he produced the killer punch when the pressure was greatest. In the last round, locked in combat with none other than Jack Nicklaus, Player watched the American blast a wood from an unlikely spot clean over the Spectacles bunkers to the fourteenth green. The South African followed by hammering one of his own to within two feet of the hole – an eagle against Nicklaus' birdie. Player later said of the shot: "It was so straight, I had to lean sideways to see the pin."

That put Player three shots clear of Nicklaus, who had done his cause no good by hooking his drive out of bounds at the long sixth. However, even that margin was scant comfort, for Nicklaus reacted with an exhibition of power golf that would have demoralised many a lesser being. The vital birdies wouldn't come, however, and Player, though dropping a shot at the sixteenth, sealed things with a scrambled 5 at the last. His 73 gave him a 289 total and saw him home by two from Nicklaus and Bob Charles, who'd been well placed before fading to a 76.

Gary Player – 1968

1975

The Tom Watson era began at Carnoustie in 1975. The man from Kansas City, who had never played a British links course, arrived with barely time for a couple of holes of practice. So, placing his fate in the hands of his caddie, Alfie Fyles, off he went and won the Open.

He knew the course by the time he'd finished, for he had to go an extra 18 holes before overcoming the Australian, Jack Newton, in a play-off, the two having tied on 279. Watson booked his place by laying his second to the last fifteen feet from the hole and securing the birdie, while Newton, who'd equalled Cotton's championship record with a 65 in his third round, needed a par 4 and duly got it.

The pursuing pack had come to grief over the finish, Nicklaus wounded by a bogey 4 at the sixteenth, Johnny Miller by a disaster in a bunker at the last. Bobby Cole of South Africa, the third-round leader by one from Newton, dropped shots at the fourteenth, fifteenth and seventeenth, but still came to the home hole needing a birdie to make the play-off, put his second four feet away and missed the putt. The three finished tied on 280.

The play-off did nothing to separate the combatants until the last hole, when, in the steady rain which had begun to fall, Newton bunkered his second and couldn't get down from 15 feet. Watson's solid par was enough. He had won his first major, the first of his five Opens, and was firmly set on the path to golfing immortality.

For Newton, a dashing golfer of immense

Tom Watson – 1975

talent, the future was to take a tragic turn at Sydney Airport in 1983 when he walked into an aircraft propeller and lost an arm and an eye. Showing wonderful spirit, he has maintained his links with the game as a television commentator and, disability or no, still plays a mean game of golf.

STEVE ELKINGTON

AUSTRALIA

BORN
8TH DECEMBER 1962, INVERELL AUSTRALIA

MAJORS
USPGA 1995

CARNOUSTIE
HOLE BY HOLE

by Keith Mackie

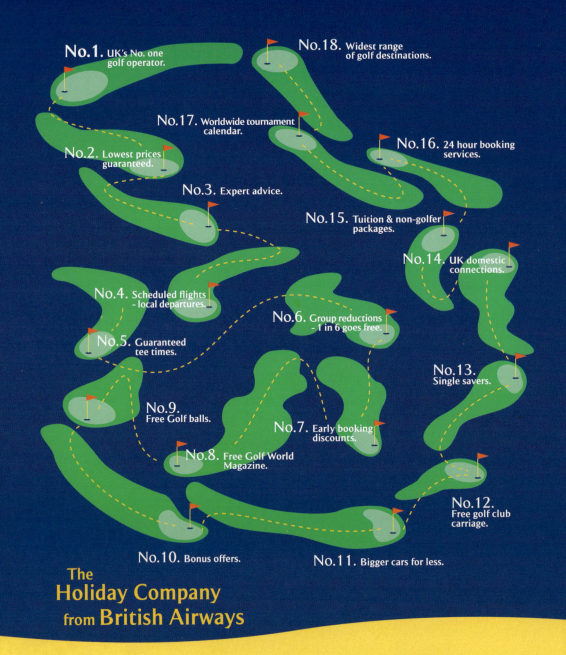

19 reasons why we are No.1.

No.19. Most of our customers book with us again. We think the others are still stuck at the 19th hole.

Call 24 hours a day for your **Club Golf** brochure.

0870 602 4000

and quote reference number CG114

www.baholidays.co.uk

ABTA V1055 ATOL 2001

407 YARDS – PAR 4

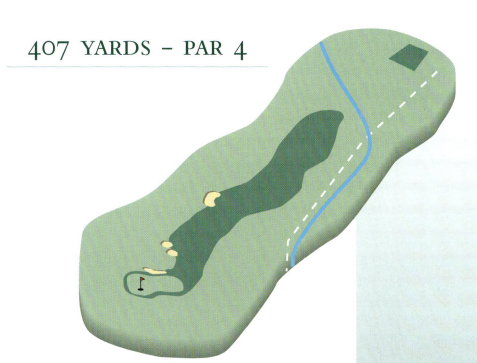

An opening tee shot into the high left side of the fairway gives a clear view of the sunken green beyond a ridge which is deeply bunkered on the right and covered in wild rough on the left. A drive falling away to the right leaves a blind approach. Against the prevailing south-west wind Ben Hogan hit a two-iron second shot in the first round of the 1953 Open.

JUSTIN LEONARD

UNITED STATES
BORN
15TH JUNE 1972, DALLAS, TEXAS

MAJORS
THE OPEN 1997

462 YARDS – PAR 4

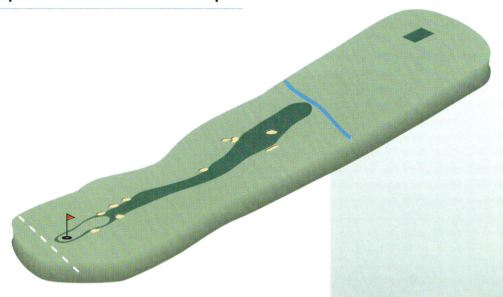

B raid's bunker in the middle of the fairway should be passed with ease by today's long-hitting players as the valley fairway turns gently to the right between large sandhills. The long, narrow green, which measures more than 50 yards from front to back, is guarded down both flanks by sand and rough and presents a difficult target.

Since it started we haven't missed one.

The Royal Bank of Scotland is proud to be the exclusive supplier of banking services to The Open Championship.

The Royal Bank of Scotland plc. Registered Office: 36 St. Andrew Square, Edinbrugh EH2 2YB. Registered in Scotland No. 90312.

342 YARDS – PAR 4

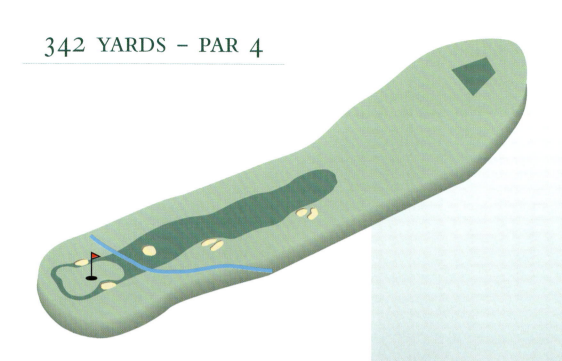

The shortest par four on the course, but a classic links hole where accuracy is the key. High sand dunes run down the right, with bunkers and Jockie's Burn on the opposite side. A long-iron from the elevated tee into the left side of the fairway will set up a wedged approach over the burn as it sweeps unseen across the face of the small, sharply contoured green.

Graeme Storm

GREAT BRITAIN

BORN
13th March 1978, Hartlepool, England
Amateur Champion 1999

412 YARDS – PAR 4

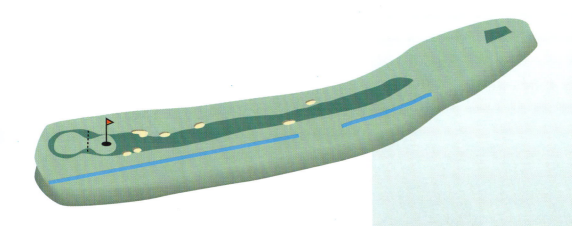

A long carry into the prevailing wind is required to clear the bunker at the corner of the dog-leg, but play too safely to the left and a ditch waits not many paces into the rough. The flat green is well protected by bunkers at the front. This is Carnoustie's only double green, shared with the 14th, although the putting surface rises into a sharp ridge between the two flags.

Mizuno - Official Workshop to the European PGA Tour, The Open Championship and Ryder Cup Matches.

Iron Count 1999 - Up to and including the German Open

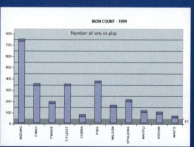

figures based on SMS research.

Mizuno 1999 European PGA Tour team

AFFLECK Paul	England	LANNER Mats	Sweden
ARRUTI Jesus	Spain	LUNA Santiago	Spain
BAKER Peter	England	MACKENZIE Malcolm	England
BEAL Andrew	England	McHENRY John	Ireland
BINAGHI Alberto	Italy	McLARDY Andrew	South Africa
BRAND Jnr. Gordon	Scotland	MOULAND Mark	Wales
CHAPMAN Roger	England	ORR Gary	Scotland
CLAYDON Russell	England	OWEN Greg	England
COCERES José	Argentina	PINERO Manuel	Spain
DAVIS Mark	England	PRICE Phillip	Wales
DRUMMOND Ross	Scotland	RAITT Andrew	England
EDLUND Dennis	Sweden	RIVERO José	Spain
GÖGELE Thomas	Germany	SHERBORNE Andrew	England
GRAPPASONNI Silvio	Italy	SINGH Jeev Milkha	India
HALLBERG Mats	Sweden	STRÜVER Sven	Germany
HANSEN Søren	Denmark	TUNNICLIFF Miles	England
HOSPITAL Domingo	Spain	WESSELS Roger	South Africa

www.mizunoeurope.com

411 YARDS – PAR 4

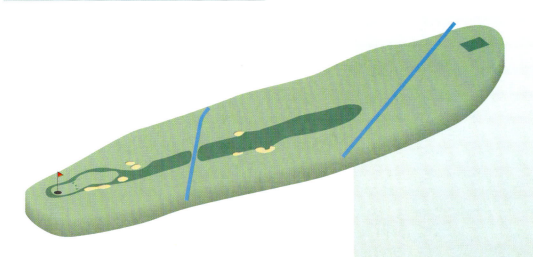

The driving line at this pronounced left-to-right dog-leg has been tightened with the addition of two bunkers in the left rough to match the one on the right. Jockie's Burn crosses at 300 yards from the tee and the 58-yard deep two-tier green cuts back at a slight angle behind more sand.

Mark Calcavecchia

UNITED STATES

BORN
12th June 1960, Laurel, Nebraska

MAJORS
The Open 1989

578 YARDS – PAR 5

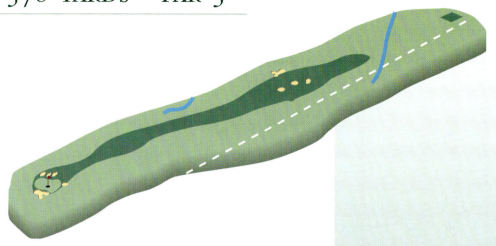

Twin bunkers in the middle of the fairway give the option of aiming for the narrow strip to the left bordered by an out-of-bounds fence all the way to the green, known since 1953 as Hogan's Alley, or the area leading into rough on the right. In the absence of a head wind long hitters have, in the past, chosen to take on the daunting carry, but a third bunker has been added 30 yards further on to make this a 300 yard plus challenge. A drainage ditch narrows the fairway 80 yards short of an angled green which has been restored to its original two-tier contours. Bunkers back and front make it a difficult target from long range.

412 YARDS – PAR 4

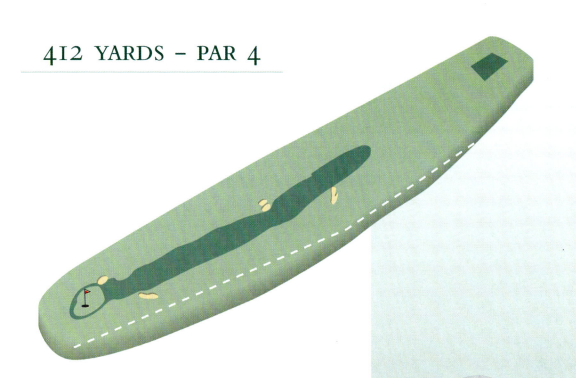

One of the more straightforward driving holes, the out-of-bounds on the left compensated by a relatively generous fairway between bunkers left and right. The small green slopes away from the player and can make downwind judgement of the second shot difficult if the wind swings to the east.

Andrew Coltart

GREAT BRITAIN

BORN
12TH MAY 1970, DUMFRIES, SCOTLAND

183 YARDS – PAR 3

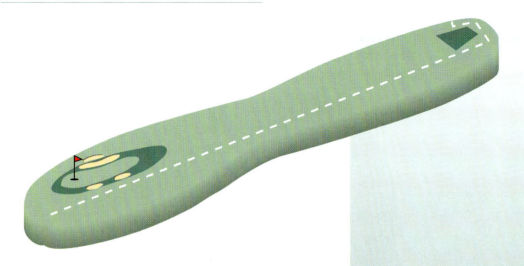

A sea of heather and gorse and a deceptive hollow at the front of the green add to the problems of club selection, especially in the prevailing left-to-right cross wind. In practice for the 1975 Open, Jack Nicklaus put his tee shot next to the hole, but playing partner Tom Weiskopf went one better and holed out with a five-iron.

USGA APPROVED

THE LAST REVOLUTION BEGINS!

**BREAKTHROUGH TECHNOLOGY THAT
HAS CHANGED THE GAME FOREVER**

Discovered at the California Institute of Technology and the winner of prestigious scientific awards in America, Liquidmetal alloy is like no other metal. When applied to golf clubs, Liquidmetal performs like no other metal and it's about to revolutionise the game.

To see and feel why Liquidmetal is now the last word in golf technology, trial a driver, an iron or a putter yourself. It will either surprise you with its power and precision off the tee or the fairway; or please you with its softness and accuracy on the green.

**There's no substitute for class, so
join the revolution from the start.**

Call 01202 201140 or fax 01202 201145 for details of a stockist near you.

LIQUIDMETAL™ PUTTER
FA-1 and FA-2

LIQUIDMETAL™ IRONS-
Set of eight

474 YARDS – PAR 4

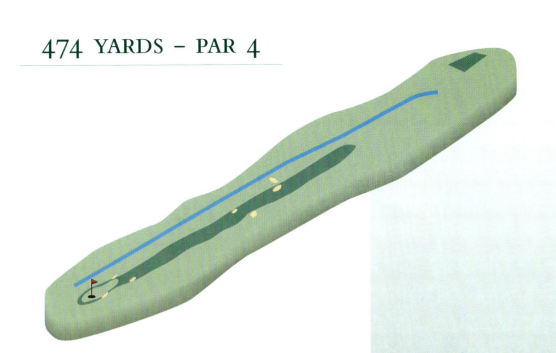

The fairway is well bunkered in the driving area and trees on the left are matched by a drainage ditch uncomfortably close in the right rough. Considerable re-shaping has been carried out in mounds and hollows around the long narrow green backed by trees and the railway line.

9

BRIAN WATTS

UNITED STATES

BORN
18TH MARCH 1966, MONTREAL, CANADA

466 YARDS – PAR 4

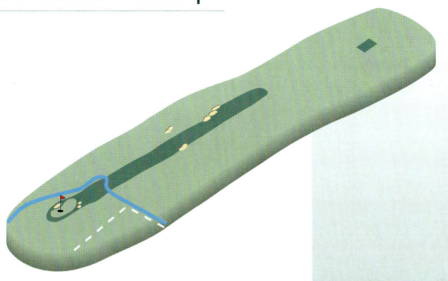

Carnoustie's second water hazard, the Barry Burn, puts in an appearance well left of the fairway and then cuts across the line of play some 30 yards short of the green and continues close to the right side of the putting surface. A nest of bunkers on the right and a lone trap on the left threaten the driving area and against an easterly wind the second shot can be as much as a wood or long iron.

Woodhall Spa

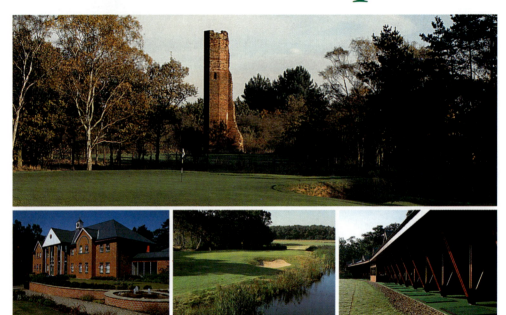

The Centre of Golfing Excellence

Visitors are always welcome to The National Golf Centre at Woodhall Spa, home of the English Golf Union, to play golf on the famous Championship Hotchkin Course (rated in the top 30 courses in the world), or the new Donald Steel designed Bracken Course - just as challenging but with a character all of its own.

- Two magnificent golf courses.
- Extensive practice facilities including a 20 bay driving range.
- Pitch and putt course set in beautiful surroundings.
- Coaching packages for all standards of golfers.
- Corporate, society days, and individual green fees welcome.
- Catering facilities for large or small groups.
- Self catering accommodation (sleeps 4) available on site.

For an information pack or special requirements call 01526 352511.

WOODHALL SPA

The English Golf Union
The National Golf Centre
The Broadway • Woodhall Spa
Lincolnshire LN10 6PU
Telephone 01526 352511
Fax 01526 351817
E-mail flint@englishgolfunion.org
Web www.englishgolfunion.org

383 YARDS – PAR 4

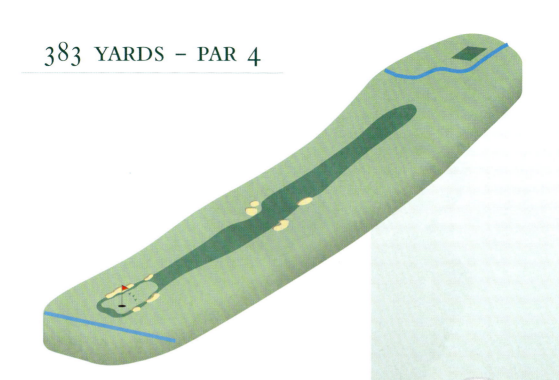

Par fours of less than 400 yards are a rarity at Carnoustie, this and the third are the only two, but lack of length is offset by a greater demand for accuracy, both from the tee and the approach to the green. Bunkers left and right of the narrow fairway restrict the driving area and the green angles away between humps and hollows and deep bunkers to offer a slim target.

11

GARY PLAYER

SOUTH AFRICA

BORN
1st November 1935, Johannesburg, South Africa

MAJORS
The Open 1959, 68, 74 • US Open 1965 • US Masters 1961, 74, 78 • USPGA 1962, 72

479 YARDS – PAR 4

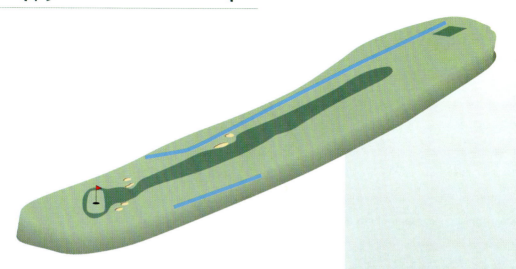

Visible bunkers and an unseen ditch on the right force tee shots to the left of the fairway. A long approach must find the gap between bunkered mounds to a green set below the level of the fairway. The putting surface is wide but shallow and a ridge splits the green into two levels with the right side being the higher.

Tom Lehman

UNITED STATES

BORN
7TH MARCH 1959, AUSTIN, MINNESOTA

MAJORS
THE OPEN 1996

169 YARDS – PAR 3

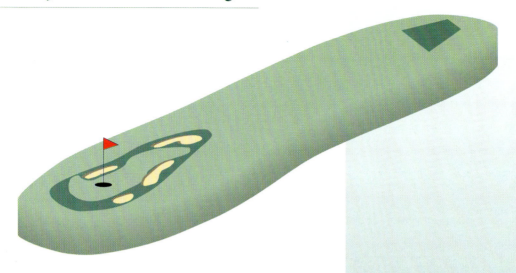

The large horse-shoe bunker which shuts off the front of the green disguises the fact that the putting surface is more than 40 yards deep and can make judgement of distance difficult. The green climbs steadily from front to back and is pinched in at midway by bunkers left and right.

13

Jesper Parnevik

SWEDEN

BORN
March 1965, Stockholm, Sweden

515 YARDS – PAR 5

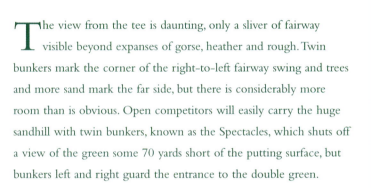

The view from the tee is daunting, only a sliver of fairway visible beyond expanses of gorse, heather and rough. Twin bunkers mark the corner of the right-to-left fairway swing and trees and more sand mark the far side, but there is considerably more room than is obvious. Open competitors will easily carry the huge sandhill with twin bunkers, known as the Spectacles, which shuts off a view of the green some 70 yards short of the putting surface, but bunkers left and right guard the entrance to the double green.

14

Davis Love III

UNITED STATES

BORN
13th April 1964,
Charlotte, North Carolina

MAJORS
USPGA 1997

472 YARDS – PAR 4

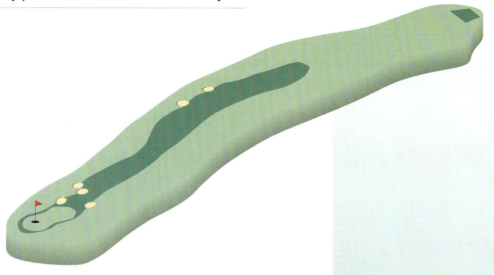

The ideal shot from the reshaped Championship tee is into the high left side of the fairway to give a clear view to the sunken green, but just off the fairway the ground tumbles away into thick rough. The sloping fairway throws the ball to the right towards bunkers and from this side the approach must carry mounds and a cluster of bunkers just short of the green.

Mark James

GREAT BRITAIN

BORN
28TH OCTOBER 1953,
MANCHESTER, ENGLAND

250 YARDS – PAR 3

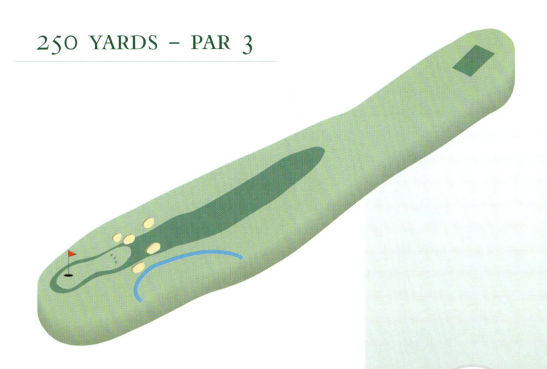

Against a north-easterly wind on the final day of the 1968 Open Jack Nicklaus was the only player to get the ball past the pin at this so-called short hole – and he used his driver. With the prevailing wind from the opposite direction the long narrow green beyond a protective ring of bunkers becomes a much easier target. Tom Watson failed to make a single par here in five rounds on his way to victory in 1975.

Jose Maria Olazabal

SPAIN

BORN
5TH FEBRUARY 1966, FUENTERRABIA, SPAIN

MAJORS
US MASTERS 1994, 99

459 YARDS – PAR 4

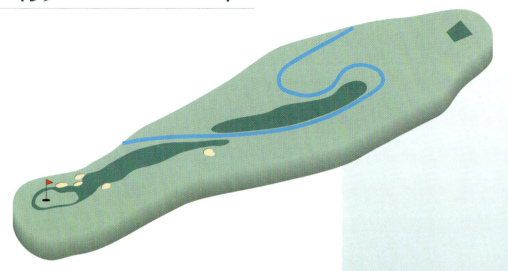

The Barry Burn loops in front of the tee, runs up the left side and cuts diagonally back across the fairway to form an island of safety between 240 and 280 yards. In the absence of a prevailing head wind longer hitters will be tempted to carry the far reaches of the water leaving only a short iron to a green which slopes down from mounds on the left to three bunkers on the right.

John Daly

UNITED STATES

BORN
28TH APRIL 1966, SACRAMENTO, CALIFORNIA

MAJORS
USPGA 1991 • THE OPEN 1995

487 YARDS – PAR 4

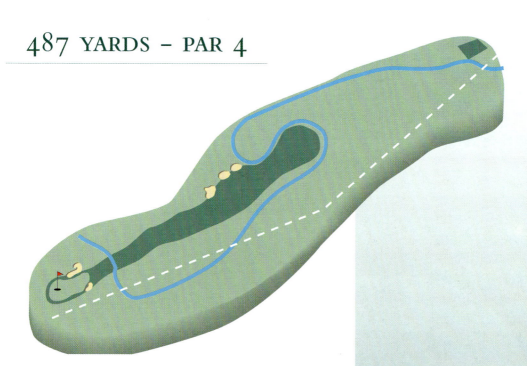

Once again the Barry Burn threatens the tee shot, running down the right, sweeping across the fairway and then looping back up the left side before disappearing out of bounds and re-emerging just short of the green. Three bunkers on the right tighten the driving line. Downwind the challenge can be reduced to a drive and short iron but against an easterly wind it will take two mightly blows to reach the home green, with out-of-bounds uncomfortably close on the left.

IF YOUR LONGEST DRIVE IS STILL NOT LONG ENOUGH..
YOU'RE READY.

INTRODUCING...
ADAMS™ SC SERIES™ TITANIUM DRIVERS
THE DRIVE REDEFINED™

Four Models, Each Designed for a Specific Swing Type...
Introducing the Adams SC Series Titanium Drivers. Not one driver. Four incredible drivers. Each model finely tuned to dramatically reduce and control distance-robbing spin. The spin that creates your slice. The spin that creates your hook. Even straight hitters benefit from the SC Series. Not only will the SC Series redefine the driver category just like Adams Tight Lies® redefined fairway woods, it will redefine your perception of distance.

Superior Spin Control for More Distance...
With painstaking precision, we milled premium Trans-Beta Forged Titanium to exact tolerances...minutely varying the asymmetry across the face. By doing so, we discovered golf's version of the Holy Grail: the first and only series of high performance drivers delivering superior spin control resulting in longer drives. Much longer. An average of six to nineteen yards longer than the three leading drivers tested.

Only from Adams...
These intricate, patent-pending designs cannot be found in any other driver made. The Adams SC Series Titanium Drivers, not bigger, not smaller, redefined.

Choose the Adams SC Series Driver designed to fit your swing...

For more information call Adams Golf
0181 947 6555

SLICE CONTROL **824 FC+**	FADE CONTROL **818 FC**	HOOK CONTROL **808 HC**	NEUTRAL **814 N**

LEADING BY DESIGN™

Adams Superior Spin Control Technology = Longer Drives

©1999 Adams Golf, Ltd. All Adams SC Series Titanium Drivers conform to USGA rules and regulations.
Patent pending on AFC technology. Adams Golf is publicly traded on the Nasdaq Stock Market National Market under the symbol ADGO.

Nick Faldo

GREAT BRITAIN

BORN

18TH JULY 1957, WELWYN GARDEN CITY, ENGLAND

MAJORS

THE OPEN 1987, 90, 92 • US MASTERS 1989, 90, 96

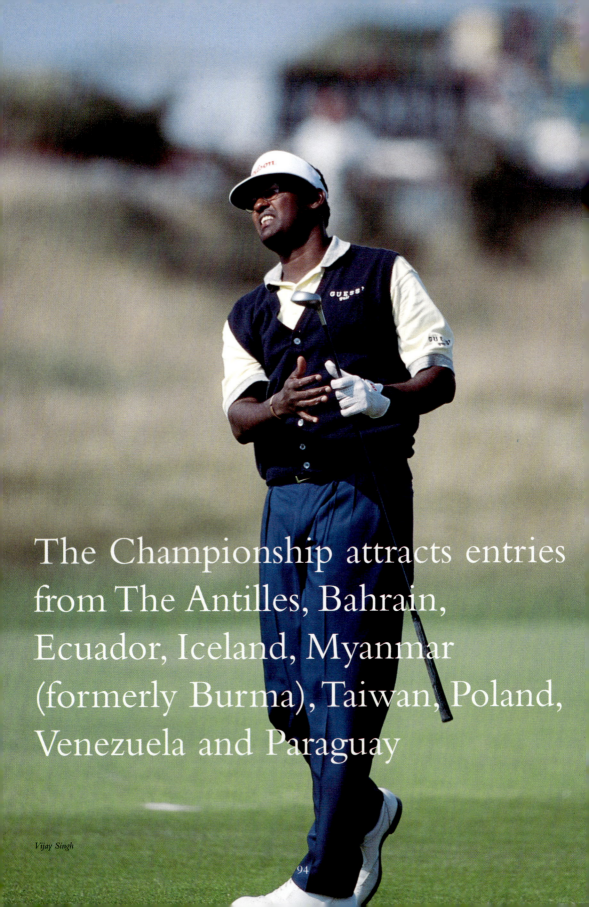

The Championship attracts entries from The Antilles, Bahrain, Ecuador, Iceland, Myanmar (formerly Burma), Taiwan, Poland, Venezuela and Paraguay

Vijay Singh

Arnold Palmer, Jack Nicklaus, Tom Watson and Lee Trevino are just four of the best from a vast army of professional golfers from the United States; Nick Faldo, Sandy Lyle and Ian Woosnam, three from the vast reservoir of golfing talent from Britain. For American and British golfers there have always been plenty of fellow countrymen on the scene but for years Bernhard Langer was Germany's one-man show on the international golfing stage. Only now is that beginning to change.

Renton Laidlaw examines the careers of players from countries which have previously had no tradition of championship golf

If Palmer revolutionised the game globally, Langer, albeit on a much smaller scale, has been a hugely impressive golfing missionary in his own country. The deeply religious 41-year-old multi-millionaire who learned his golf as a young caddie at Augsburg could claim, if he were not too modest to do so, that he single-handedly popularised the game in his country. If there are twice as many people playing golf in Germany today than at the start of the 70's and twice as many courses for them to play on, with more on the way to meet demand, it can be attributed to twice Masters Champion Langer's achievements on the world stage.

Today he is not the only German professional on Tour with a well-stamped passport. Talented younger Germans are trying to outscore Langer who continues, despite having recovered three times from the yips and a serious back complaint, to hit some of the crispest and most accurate approach irons of anyone in golf. Sven Struver, Alex Cejka, originally from Marienbad in the Czech Republic, and Thomas Gogele point to Langer as their inspiration just as a host of young Spaniards insist that Seve Ballesteros was their hero, all young Italian Tour professionals have been encouraged by the global feats of Costantino Rocca and young British golfers look up to six-times major winner Faldo.

Winning golf tournaments is all about heart, guts and talent – something some lucky people may be born with but, for most, success is the end product of long hours on the range and practice putting green, hitting balls and perfecting a reliable swing and putting stroke. In this department Langer is on the short list for the hardest worker on Tour. Just ask caddie Coleman who, mischievously, suggested recently that Bernhard's excellent score in one round of a European Tour event was the result of his not having been able to practise for as long as normal the day before because of a niggling injury. Langer was aware of the inference but resumed his normal punishing practice schedule when he was again fully fit!

Sven Struver

Today Langer, like Jack Nicklaus, is leaving a legacy of excellently designed courses, many in his own homeland, but he is conscious that the increased awareness of the game in Germany does not yet stretch to the less wealthy in the population. For too many Germans there are still not enough courses on which they can easily get a game at a reasonable price despite the remarkable Langer-inspired boom.

Golf course design is an area in which reigning USPGA Championship title holder Vijay Singh also dabbles with the one he has been asked to design in his native Fiji giving him particular pleasure. His new course will be a much-needed Championship test and it is bound to have a huge practice range!

If Langer was, for a long time, a one-man oom-pah-pah band in Germany, Singh has certainly been that in the sun-drenched islands he calls home. Of Indian extraction, Singh, who has a real passion for the game, learned to play while caddying for his father at the course close by Fiji's international airport where Mr Singh senior worked. Vijay is, in fact, Fiji's only international superstar – and this time the description superstar is fully valid.

When Vijay won his first major at Sahalee last year with a last gasp triumph over Steve Stricker he was realising a dream which, for a time when languishing as a club professional in Borneo, might have appeared impossible. Yet his older brother Krishna never faltered in his confidence that Vijay would some day win one of those four coveted major titles. He knew his brother's immense love of and dedication to the game and knew his desire and determination were massively positive factors in his long battle to reach the top.

If Singh himself has justifiable pride in what he

Bernhard Langer

has achieved he knows the Fijians are equally impressed by their golfing hero's performances around the world. He really has been a "have clubs will travel" operator winning titles in places as diverse as Nigeria and Sweden, Zimbabwe and Spain, the Ivory Coast and Italy, Malaysia and America, South Africa, France and Germany.

The golf scene in Fiji may be changing but, just as in Langer's Germany, many of Singh's greatest fans cannot afford to join a club. In Fiji the game still suffers from a certain exclusivity but it has not stopped Dinesh Chand, the youngster who used to caddy for Vijay, making the grade with the help of a wealthy sponsor from Japan. Indeed, he has already done what Vijay Singh has still to do – post a victory on the Japanese circuit. Suddenly there is another Fijian on the world stage. Singh may have Fijian company in this week's Championship if Chand survives the pressure-packed final qualifying.

The Open has always been the most

Carlos Franco

international of the four majors – a fact underlined again this year with forty-seven countries having representatives in the field for Carnoustie. Some of those golfers will not survive regional or final qualifying but the fact that the Championship attracts entries from The Antilles, Bahrain, Ecuador, Iceland, Myanmar (formerly Burma), Taiwan, Poland, Venezuela and Paraguay is impressive by any standards and had Stephen Ames not withdrawn, there would have been a lone representative from Trinidad and Tobago. The fact that Trevor Dodds, a winner on the US tour, did not enter means Namibia will have nobody at Carnoustie.

There might have been a Chinese golfer too but that country's top man Zhang Lian-Wei, who often has to convince passport and visa officials not only that he is a golf professional but what that means, pulled out a few weeks ago. These days China is embracing golf so enthusiastically that they are even claiming their Emperors invented the game long before the St Andrews shepherds thought up the idea!

Among the most successful professionals from countries where the game is still ultra elite and seldom makes the sports pages is the Paraguayan Carlos Franco. The population of Paraguay is four million, of whom only an estimated 300 play golf regularly, mostly at Ascuncion Golf Club where Franco's late father was a greenkeeper. Carlos and his five brothers are all professionals but Carlos is the star. When Paraguay were drawn against Scotland in the 1993 Alfred Dunhill Cup at St Andrews Colin Montgomerie famously suggested that if he and his two team-mates could not beat the Paraguayans, then Scotland should not be in the competition. Paraguay won 2-1 with Carlos Franco, inspired throughout his career by Jack Nicklaus and Seve Ballesteros, scoring a four shot victory over Sam Torrance.

Last December, at tricky Royal Melbourne, Franco, a member of the Japanese Tour before gaining his US card, played outstandingly good golf for the International side that surprised a maybe too complacent US team in the President's Cup and when the moustachioed South American came sixth in this year's US Masters behind winner Jose Maria Olazabal, he was given a hero's welcome on his return home. Goodness knows how the locals reacted when Franco, who speaks Spanish, Japanese to his caddie, Paraguayan Guarani and ever-improving English, won the US Tour's Compaq Classic in New Orleans in May.

Franco, who used to caddie for $3 as a child, is now a dollar millionaire supporting over 30 relatives and majestically putting Paraguay on the golfing map. What a fairy-tale it would be if the swashbuckling Señor were to win the final Open Championship of the Millennium.

# FORE.

THE FAMOUS GROUSE
EXCLUSIVE SUPPLIER TO THE OPEN CHAMPIONSHIP

PHIL MICKELSON

UNITED STATES

BORN
16TH JUNE 1970, SAN DIEGO, CALIFORNIA

Retief Goosen

SOUTH AFRICA

BORN

8TH FEBRUARY 1969, PIETERSBERG, SOUTH AFRICA

"He never showed emotion either but he certainly never showed any weakness."

Ben Hogan and wife, Valerie

Would Ben Hogan have become the admired and feared golfer if his life had taken a different turn? Would he have become the man against whom every golfer of the modern era – and by that is meant postwar – is measured if he had not suffered two extraordinary traumas, one when he was a small child, the other when he was a grown man, perhaps at the peak of his career?

To almost every golfer born in and since the 1950s, growing up was no more difficult than facing a series of short uphill putts. Few can have experienced anything approaching hardship the way Hogan did. Times were difficult in the Hogan

> *John Hopkins, of The Times, discusses the career of one of golf's greats – Ben Hogan, winner at Carnoustie in 1953*

household when Ben was born, the third of three children, on 13th August 1912. They were to get much worse. Chester Hogan, Ben's father, was a depressive, who endured his handicap in silence. He drank and at times was unable to work. When Ben was nine, Chester Hogan could cope no more. Early one evening he put a .38 revolver into his chest and shot himself.

It is not known whether it was Ben who was in the room with his father at this horrible moment or whether it was Royal, Ben's older brother, who was 14. The *Fort Worth Record* reported that a six-year-old son was playing on the floor of the room. *The Dublin Progress* reported that Royal entered the room and seeing his father searching in a grip asked: "Daddy, what are you going to do?"

Whether Ben or Royal saw their father kill himself or whether they heard the shattering noise of a gunshot when they were in an adjoining room scarcely diminishes the awfulness of what happened. Goodness knows the effect this had on the young Ben Hogan but the effect on the family's finances is easy to imagine. There had not been very much money before.

There was even less now. Ben, the second son and third child, began to sell newspapers after school, sometimes taking most of the night to get rid of his stock, and then he started caddying while Clara his mother took a job as a seamstress. Hogan had to cope with being taunted for his size. He had to work hard to earn money to contribute to the family coffers, often having to use his fists to fight for the best positions at railway stations from which to sell his papers. Hogan may have stopped using his fists soon after this but he never stopped fighting.

In 1949 he and Valerie, his wife, were driving their Cadillac on a foggy morning in Texas and crashed into a bus that was overtaking the vehicle in front and was temporarily on the wrong side of the road. As the bus appeared in front of them, Hogan threw himself across the front seats to protect Valerie. This move reduced the injuries she suffered and saved his life. The car's steering column was impaled on the now empty driver's seat. Hogan's left ankle, leg and shoulder were shattered, his pelvis and several ribs broken. It was $1\frac{1}{2}$ hours before an ambulance arrived. Hogan spent two months in hospital and nearly died from blood clots in his legs.

Hogan was as determined to regain his strength and golfing prowess as he had been to earn money as a little boy. He did numerous exercises in hospital to regain his strength. He had to learn to walk again. Barely six months after this horrific accident he began to hit balls.

"Some time that fall he told me he wanted to go out to the club," Valerie Hogan recalled in an interview with Ron Sirak of the American magazine *Golf World* earlier this year. "I said we could go but that he could only look. He said 'No, I'm going to take some of my clubs'. I was really worried that he was trying to get back too soon. He just said: 'this is something I've got to do.' I had my doubts he would make it because I did not know if he knew how badly he'd been hurt. All I told him was not to expect too much, and not to be too hard on himself, but I might as well have been speaking to a chair. He was determined he was going to do it. He had no doubts."

Determined he was going to do it. No doubts. These are the words of the person closest to him, the person who would know if he showed any weakness. Hogan did not. He never showed emotion either but he certainly never showed any weakness.

Can you imagine what he must have gone

Ben Hogan at Carnoustie in 1953

through simply to get back on to his feet and start walking again? Can you imagine the determination he must have shown in the first tournament in which he competed after his accident, which he only lost in a play-off to Sam Snead? But consider this. He won more major championships after his accident than before, perhaps the most famous coming in the 1950 US Open at Merion 16 months after his dreadful accident, including playing 36 holes in one day. He won his first major championship in 1946, the PGA Championship, and two more before his accident and six after it, including the three in that momentous year, 1953.

The speed of Hogan's recovery was that of a man intent upon making up for lost time. Why? Because that was how he was at everything. Whether on the golf course or off it, Hogan appeared to be driven by a raging fury. He had a work ethic that was exceptional. He was too busy for small talk, too intent upon looking down the fairway to assess the next stroke, too driven to demonstrate any frivolity.

I believe the death of his father and the car accident in 1949 shaped Hogan's life because those two events had scored themselves into his consciousness and taught him that without work very little was achievable but with it he could do almost anything. "Ben worked harder than any golf professional I've ever known and from what others say, harder than anyone anybody else has ever known," Valerie Hogan said.

We started this article by posing two questions. The answer to these questions should have become clear by now but in case it hasn't here it is. It comes from the horse's mouth. "I don't think I could have done what I've done if I hadn't had the tough days to begin with," Ben Hogan said.

Tom Watson

United States

Born
4th September 1949, Kansas City, Missouri

Majors
The Open 1975, 77, 80, 82, 83 • US Open 1982 • US Masters 1977, 81

Greg Norman

Australia

Born
10th February 1955, Queensland, Australia

Majors
The Open 1986, 93

The Perfect Round

Exclusive supplier to the 1999 Open Golf Championship

Fred Couples

UNITED STATES

BORN
3RD OCTOBER 1959, SEATTLE, WASHINGTON

MAJORS
US MASTERS 1992

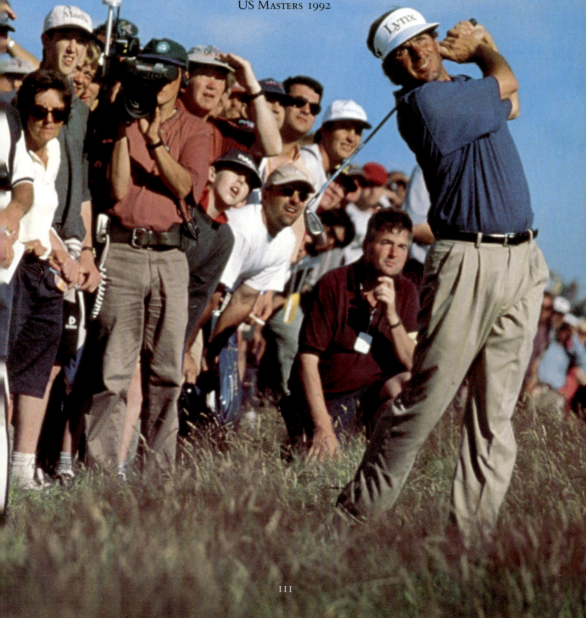

GOLF FOUNDATION

Come and see us in the

Schweppes Junior Golf Tent

Free Golf Lessons for Juniors
Book a free 15-minute lesson with a PGA Professional.

Daily Prize Draw
Buy a raffle ticket for just £1 and you could win a superb prize.

Photographs of Top Players
Professional high gloss photographs of your favourite players are available.

Putting competition
When the pressure's on can you hold your nerve?

Information Desk
Staff are available to answer your questions about any of the Golf Foundation's activities.

Something for everyone!
Autograph books and marker pens, practice balls and much more!

" I received invaluable help from the Golf Foundation as a youngster."
Lee Westwood

WHAT WE DO

Coaching
- Starter Centre Initiative
- Merit Award Scheme
- School/Youth Group Coaching Scheme
- Special Needs Coaching Scheme
- Club Coaching Scheme
- Junior Golf Leaders Award

Tournaments
- Weetabix Age Group Championships
- Team Championship for Schools
- Adult/Junior Foursomes

Visit our web-site at
www.golf-foundation.org

GOLF FOUNDATION
Supporting Junior Golf
The National Body for the Development of Junior Golf
Registered Charity Number 285917

"By supporting the Golf Foundation you are helping to safeguard the future of the sport."
Bernard Gallacher
President of the Golf Foundation

николас price

ZIMBABWE

BORN
28TH JANUARY 1957, DURBAN, SOUTH AFRICA

MAJORS
USPGA 1992, 94 • THE OPEN 1994

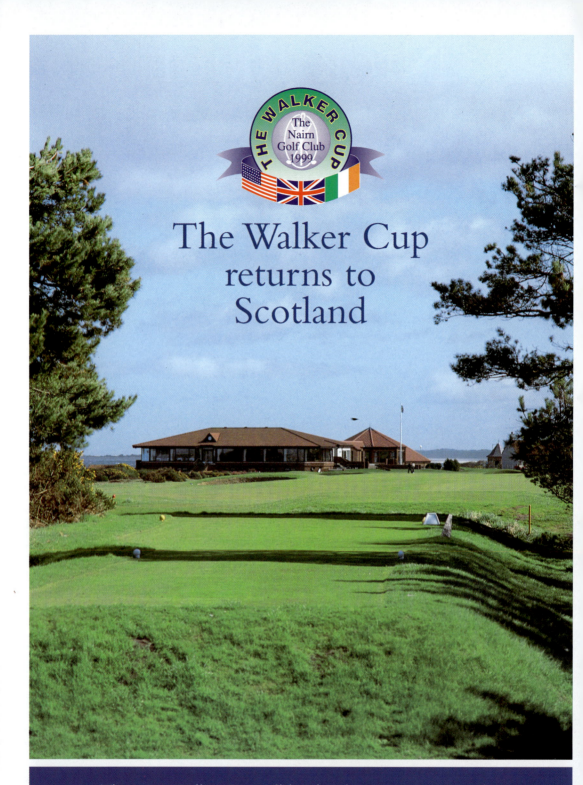

The Walker Cup returns to Scotland

This year's Walker Cup will be played at Nairn in September. Scott Crockett looks at recent matches between GB&I and the USA

The cream of amateur golfing talent from both sides of the Atlantic will gather for the first time in the north of Scotland at Nairn in September, having last met north of the border at Muirfield in 1979 when the Americans ran out comfortable $15\frac{1}{2}$ - $8\frac{1}{2}$ victors over Great Britain & Ireland.

Reports of an American success should not come as a surprise for, in the 77-year history of the biennial contest, they hold an overwhelming 31-4 advantage with one match tied at Baltimore in 1965.

But the omens for victory for the home side are good this year as there was a strong Scottish influence in their previous four successes.

GB&I's first win came at St Andrews in 1938 and the second was also on the Old Course in 1971. Their only victory to date in America, at Peachtree in 1989, was sealed by Jim Milligan of Kilmarnock (Barassie) while four Scots – Gordon Sherry, Stephen Gallacher, Barclay Howard and Graham Rankin – played their part in the 14-10 win at Royal Porthcawl in 1995.

Sadly, flanking those memorable two days in South Wales are two heavy defeats on American soil, a 19-5 thrashing at Interlachen in 1993 followed by an 18-6 reverse in the last match at Quaker Ridge in 1997.

All hope of continuing the feelgood factor of Royal Porthcawl was dashed in a disastrous opening session at the Scarsdale course in New York State two years ago, the Americans winning all four foursomes to open up a mathematical and psychological gap which was never closed.

Three and a half points out of eight for GB&I in the afternoon's singles saw the deficit widen to five and when another 3-1 reverse in the second day's foursomes moved the Americans' overall points advantage to seven with only eight singles remaining, it was all over bar the shouting.

Young Scot Steven Young halted the celebrations momentarily with his second singles win at the top of the order, this time a 2&1 victory over Joel Kribel, having a day earlier beaten Duke Delcher 5&4, while fellow countryman Craig Watson did his bit with a square game against Jason Gore in the second tie.

But the inevitable American onslaught arrived with a vengeance and without having to go to the last green, the home side took all six remaining singles for a resounding victory.

Although naturally disappointed, time moved on and GB&I gave themselves the perfect fillip for this year's match with victory last November in the World Amateur Team Championship in Chile.

A strong American side, headed by US Masters hero Matt Kuchar, arrived in Santiago fully optimistic they could win the Eisenhower Trophy and in the process erase the painful memory of their ninth place finish in Manila in 1996, the USA's worst ever performance and indeed only the third time they had finished outside the top two.

But they had not reckoned with the strength and all round ability of the GB&I quartet, Englishmen Luke Donald and Gary Wolstenholme, Scot Lorne Kelly and Irishman Paddy Gribben, the 1998 European Individual Amateur Champion.

Inspired by non-playing captain Peter McEvoy, GB&I broke out of a 3rd round triple tie for second place with defending champions Australia and the USA to overhaul long-time leaders Finland and win by four strokes.

Their final round total of 208 comprised a sparkling four-under-par 67 by Wolstenholme, a

70 by Kelly and a 71 by Donald – a superb team effort under great pressure which lifted them clear of the field at six-under-par 852.

Australia completed a courageous defence of their title in the runners-up position with Chinese Taipei grabbing a surprise third, while the Americans slumped to seventh place after a disappointing final day aggregate of 221.

It was GB&I's fourth Eisenhower Trophy victory since the tournament started at St Andrews in 1958 but the first outside Europe following victories in Italy (1964), Portugal (1976) and Sweden (1988).

"It was a fantastic performance with the pressure on," said captain McEvoy who played in the last GB&I team to win eleven years ago in Ullna where he also took the individual title.

"All the lads played well when it came to the crunch and I'm very proud of them. Also don't let anyone fool you that it is more difficult to be a non-playing captain than it is to be a player – I had the easy job on the sidelines."

That was not an opinion shared by veteran Wolstenholme who paid tribute to his captain and who will be keen to make his third appearance in the Walker Cup this year, his first in 1995 crowned by a memorable last green singles victory over Tiger Woods.

"We had a great team spirit going and I must pay tribute to the part Peter McEvoy played," said Gary. "In the last round he was haring backwards and forwards between all four of us, full of enthusiasm and encouragement and keeping us right up to date about what we needed to do. He was immense."

Such insight suggests McEvoy might adopt the Seve Ballesteros-style of captaincy come the match itself and he will be acquainted with every blade of grass his buggy zooms over come September, thanks to the meticulous preparation

The victorious GB&I Team at Royal Porthcawl, 1995

by the GB&I team.

Introduced in 1995, the squad system has already seen a group of top players visit Nairn twice for training weekends, with another session taking place in late August after the team has been selected.

While anticipated that most of the team will come from the current squad of 23, other players are not ruled out of consideration for selection if they perform well throughout the season, as Graham Rankin did to make the side in 1995.

The make up of the American team depends very much on whether star turns such as Kuchar decide to turn professional but history has shown that whichever ten represent the Stars and Stripes, captain Danny Yates, the 48-year-old Georgian who played on the losing side at Peachtree in 1989 and on the winning side at Interlachen four years later, will have a wealth of talent at his disposal.

Although the Walker Cup is a first for Nairn and the north of Scotland, the 112-year-old links is no stranger to top level competition in both the amateur and professional spheres.

Its association with the R&A has seen it play host to the Boys Internationals and Championship in 1989 as well as the Amateur Championship in 1994 when England's Lee James beat Gordon Sherry 2&1.

It has hosted numerous Northern Opens on the Tartan Tour, the Scottish Amateur Stroke Play Championship in 1975 where Charlie Green was victorious and the 1987 Scottish Amateur Championship where Colin Montgomerie thrashed Alasdair Watt 9&8 to win the title before embarking on his mercurial rise in the professional ranks.

Nairn's golfing credentials were enhanced in 1990 with the opening of a new clubhouse which affords a marvellous view over the links and the rolling Moray Firth to the distant Black Isle.

The US Walker Cup Team, winners at Quaker Ridge in 1997

Discover one of Yorkshire's hidden treasures...

Aldwark Manor Hotel, Golf & Country Club... *truly a golf lover's paradise*

Set within a beautiful mature parkland estate, the 18-hole golf course offers a superb playing experience. Every hole is bordered by ancient oak and beech trees with the meandering river Ure regularly coming into play to provide golfers of all levels with an exciting challenge.

The Manor is the perfect setting for corporate and society golf events, able to cater for all levels of hospitality. It boasts a fine dining restaurant, a splendid new golfer's Spike Bar and a delightful alfresco dining terrace where one can watch the returning golfers playing to the 18th green. To complete the picture there are 27 en suite bedrooms including a number of new, inexpensive 'overnight golfer' rooms. Aldwark Manor offers everything the discerning golfer could wish for.

A full range of golf event packages are available along with country, overseas and corporate memberships.

Why not attend a residential golf school at Aldwark Manor or use us as a base to sample other great golf courses and attractions within the vale of York? Our Director of Golf will be happy to advise on event planning, suitable memberships and special bespoke touring trips.

We are well situated on the main A1(M) north-south route and are within easy reach of both rail and air networks, where collection by our mini-coach can be arranged.

If you love golf, you are sure to love Aldwark Manor.

We look forward to seeing you very soon.

To receive a *free* copy of our new colour brochure call now on +44 (0)1347 838146

BIGGA
Home of BIGGA, the British & International Golf Greenkeepers Association

ALDWARK MANOR
HOTEL, GOLF & COUNTRY CLUB
Aldwark, Near Alne, York, YO61 1UF United Kingdom

Hotel Tel: +44 (0)1347 838146   Hotel Fax: +44 (0)1347 838867   Golf Tel: +44 (0)1347 838353   Golf Fax: +44 (0)1347 830007

PAYNE STEWART

UNITED STATES

BORN
30th January 1957, Springfield, Missouri

MAJORS
USPGA 1989 • US Open 1991, 99

The other fairways of the Open Championship

by George Makey, MBE

The "Golf Masters Anonymous" crusade, founded in 1975 has, so far, raised £3.8 million to bring the magical independence of powered mobility to brighten the lives of needy youngsters and of their families.

In this total over the last 12 years, under the banner of 'The Peter Alliss Masters', £1,850,000 has been raised to provide powered wheelchairs for mainly UK youngsters, but also for some as widely spread as New Zealand, USA and South Africa. Every single £ raised goes towards providing those powered wheelchairs which open up a whole new life to disadvantaged youngsters.

Every Open Championship since 1977 has provided the setting for the presentation of the wheelchairs. Including the 14 to be presented this year, 175 needy youngsters have benefited from the generosity of the 'Peter Alliss Masters' supporters to the tune of £280,000.

This year's generous donors are:
THE KEEPERS OF THE GREEN
- Neal Garland (Founder Life Member), Longview, Texas, USA
- KOTG per Sandy Mitchell (SPAR) Ceres, Fife & Dundee University (NY Marathon)
- Midsummer's Unlikely G.S., Edinburgh (2)
- Sportsman's Charity, Edinburgh
- Kevin Doyle, Caledonian Heritable Ltd, Edinburgh
- World Professional Billiards and Snooker Association

THE PETER ALLISS MASTERS
- The R&A Championship Committee
- Royal Blackheath Golf Club
- British Turkey Federation (2)
- Peppi Pollio, Cooden Beach
- 3 Rivers G.&C.C., Chelmsford
- Craw's Nest Hotel, Anstruther, Fife
- Sportsman's Charity, Edinburgh

TOTAL: 15 POWERED WHEELCHAIRS

The Spirit of AULD TOM MORRIS back at the Open Championship

Auld Tom Morris, universally regarded as 'The Grand Old Man of Golf', was born and bred in St Andrews (1821-1908). Historians of the game rate him as probably the greatest golfer of all time. He was four times Open Champion in 1861, 1862, 1864 and 1867.

He moved to Prestwick in 1851 where he was known as the Keeper of the Green. In 1860 Auld Tom was the runner-up in the inaugural Open Championship at Prestwick. He returned to his beloved St Andrews in 1864 as Professional, responsible for the Old Course, at a salary of £50 per annum. There, for the next forty years he nurtured and improved the hallowed links in his own inimitable fashion. He also developed a club making business in his shop overlooking the 18th green, subsequently named after him; and the Tom Morris shop stands there to this very day.

He was a family man and a devout Christian who read his Bible every day and would never play 'gowf' on a Sunday. He set high standards of performance and behaviour on and off the course. Come sun or snow he took a daily dip in the waters of St Andrews Bay.

Today his plaque, on the facing wall of the Clubhouse of the Royal and Ancient Golf Club of St Andrews, gives him the perfect view of the first fairway towards the Swilken Burn as he watches every opening drive. He sometimes gives a wry smile as he watches the modern-day golfer playing in and out of the Valley of Sin just short of the 18th green – the 'Tom Morris' hole.

18th December 1995 saw the inauguration of the first on-going golfing tribute to Auld Tom Morris, when, Sir Michael Bonallack, Secretary of the R&A, presented the first ever 'Keepers of the Green' powered wheelchair to 54-year-old Crawford Welch from St Andrews.

'Keepers of the Green' golf can only be played with just five hickory clubs, authentic reproductions of those designed, made and used by Auld Tom Morris over 100 years ago and hand-crafted by Barry Kerr in his St Andrews workshop. These clubs are exclusive to Life Members – enrolled in the 'spirit' of Auld Tom. The registered ownership of these 'hickories' gives the Life Member an automatic invitation to play in any 'KOTG' event across the international boundaries. These unique clubs are not available to the general public. Life Membership (by invitation) fee for 1999 is £550 for clubs and matching bag.

We currently have Life Members in the UK, USA and Sweden. Annual programmes are being developed in separate States of USA and in other countries or Islands to mirror-image those already established in the UK. Such national programmes are authorised by the governing body of 'Keepers of the Green' in St Andrews just as soon as 24 Life Members are enrolled in each territory and registered in St Andrews.

The Annual Auld Tom Morris World Memorial Championship will always be played in St Andrews on one of those courses built by Auld Tom and the Annual Auld Tom Morris East Neuk Championship over the Balcomie Links of Crail, converted by him in 1895. International 'Keepers of the Green' golf is played under the auspices of the governing body deeply rooted in St Andrews – to provide powered mobility for the needy of all ages – in the 'spirit' of **Auld Tom Morris**!

Tom Morris

OCS Group
Managers of the Essentials

The OCS Group is the UK's leading independent property support services group, providing all the essential ingredients for cleanliness, safety, hygiene and total security throughout your premises.

With more than forty specialist companies, the OCS Group offers the highest level of service

covering office and window cleaning, washroom hygiene, M&E maintenance, laundry, security, lighting maintenance, indoor plant displays, landscape maintenance and many others.

For full details about how we can help your company call our hotline now - 0171 498 0088

Managing the Essentials

OCS Group Ltd 44 South Side Clapham Common London SW4 9BU
Tel: 0171 498 0088   Fax: 0171 498 6871   Email: group.marketing@dial.pipex.com   Web Site: http://www.ocs-group.com

Jarmo Sandelin

SWEDEN

BORN
10th May 1967, Imatra, Finland

NORTHERN IRELAND...

...famous for its links

Senior British Open Championship
at
Royal Portrush Golf Club
22–25 July 1999

IT'S EASY to get to Northern Ireland - with over 22 airport departure points from Great Britain, and from 3 main car ferry ports during most of the year - 5 in the summer! It's even easier travelling from the Republic of Ireland. Once you arrive in Northern Ireland, the course of your dreams is never more than a short drive away. There are a dozen within 5 miles of Belfast City Centre alone, and a host of others studding the spectacular shoreline or nestling in beautiful countryside. Green fees are moderate, accommodation is comfortable and affordable with a welcome that is second to none.
So, make your links to Northern Ireland. Call us today on the numbers below. For more information on the Northern Ireland Golfers Passport, call at Stand No. 17 in the tented village.

Northern Ireland Tourist Board

St Anne's Court, 59 North Street,
Belfast BT1 1NB
Tel: 01232 246609 or 0541 555 250
Internet: http://ni-tourism.com
Quoting reference OGC 99

WOULDN'T IT BE NICE IF EVERY TIME YOU STEPPED ON THE TEE THE FAIRWAY BECAME WIDER?

The Revolutionary STRAIGHT DISTANCE. The straighter the ball, the wider your fairway. The straighter the ball, the longer your distance. The straighter the ball, the shorter your hole. The straighter the ball, the better your score. The straighter the ball, the better your mood. Isn't it amazing what can happen when you reduce that ugly, distance-eating, put-you-in-the-rough side-spin. Visit us online at: www.wilsonsports.com

FOR DETAILS OF YOUR NEAREST STAFF TITANIUM STRAIGHT DISTANCE STOCKIST CALL **01294 316200** OR SEE **SKYTEXT** PAGE **284**.

Wilson® Staff
TITANIUM
LONG WITHOUT THE WRONG.™

THE OPEN CHAMPIONSHIP Prize Fund

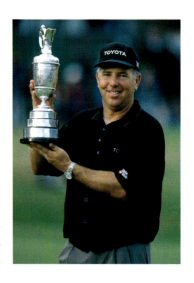

The winner will receive the Championship Gold Medal. The first Amateur in the Championship, unless he is the winner, will receive a Silver Medal provided he has completed 72 holes. Other Amateurs who complete 72 holes will each receive a Bronze Medal.

Prize Money as shown below shall be allocated to professional golfers. Any Prize Money which would have been won by an amateur golfer will be allotted to the professional golfer next in order of merit as his prize, and all subsequent place monies will be renumbered accordingly.

If any Qualifying Competition is won by an amateur golfer, he will be presented with a memento.

(a) Open Championship (subject to alteration by ties for places 2 to 156):
If more than 70 professional golfers qualify for the final two rounds, additional prize money will be added. Prize money will decrease by £50 per place from 71st and below. All qualifiers will receive a minimum of £4000.

(b) Final Qualifying Competitions In each Competition, Prize Money will be allocated to the first three places as follows: 1st £800 2nd £600 3rd £400. Professional golfers who gain reserve places in Final Qualifying Competitions will each receive £85, subject to their not being called upon to play in the Championship.

(c) Regional Qualifying Competitions In each Competition, Prize Money will be allocated to the first three places as follows: 1st £400 2nd £300 3rd £200.

Place	Prize	Place	Prize	Place	Prize	Place	Prize	Place	Prize
1	£350,000	15	£28,000	29	£13,500	43	£8,800	57	£6,800
2	£215,000	16	£26,000	30	£13,000	44	£8,600	58	£6,700
3	£155,000	17	£24,000	31	£12,500	45	£8,400	59	£6,600
4	£110,000	18	£23,000	32	£12,000	46	£8,200	60	£6,500
5	£90,000	19	£22,000	33	£11,500	47	£8,000	61	£6,450
6	£70,000	20	£21,000	34	£11,000	48	£7,850	62	£6,400
7	£55,000	21	£20,000	35	£10,600	49	£7,700	63	£6,350
8	£50,000	22	£19,000	36	£10,300	50	£7,550	64	£6,300
9	£45,000	23	£18,000	37	£10,000	51	£7,400	65	£6,250
10	£41,000	24	£17,000	38	£9,800	52	£7,300	66	£6,200
11	£37,000	25	£16,000	39	£9,600	53	£7,200	67	£6,150
12	£34,000	26	£15,000	40	£9,400	54	£7,100	68	£6,100
13	£32,000	27	£14,500	41	£9,200	55	£7,000	69	£6,050
14	£30,000	28	£14,000	42	£9,000	56	£6,900	70	£6,000

Non qualifiers after two rounds – Leading 10 professional golfers and ties £1,100; next 20 professional golfers and ties £900; next 20 professional golfers and ties £800; remainder of professional golfers and ties £700.

Bob Charles

NEW ZEALAND

BORN
14th March 1936, Carterton, New Zealand

MAJORS
The Open 1963

128th Open Golf Championship

Players who are exempt from Regional & Final Qualifying Competitions
(Correct at time of going to press)

Stephen Allan	Australia	Tom Lehman	USA
Billy Andrade	USA	Justin Leonard	USA
Stuart Appleby	Australia	Davis Love III	USA
Peter Baker	UK	Sandy Lyle	UK
Severiano Ballesteros	Spain	Andrew Magee	USA
Thomas Bjorn	Denmark	Jeff Maggert	USA
Gordon Brand Jnr.	UK	Shigeki Maruyama	Japan
Mark Brooks	USA	Billy Mayfair	USA
Mark Calcavecchia	USA	Rocco Mediate	USA
David Carter	UK	Phil Mickelson	USA
Bob Charles	New Zealand	Colin Montgomerie	UK
Stewart Cink	USA	Jarrod Moseley	Australia
Darren Clarke	UK	Frank Nobilo	New Zealand
Andrew Coltart	UK	Greg Norman	Australia
Fred Couples	USA	Mark O'Meara	USA
Ben Crenshaw	USA	Jose Maria Olazabal	Spain
John Daly	USA	Naomichi Ozaki	Japan
Glen Day	USA	Rodney Pampling	Australia
Scott Dunlap	USA	Jesper Parnevik	Sweden
David Duval	USA	Craig Parry	Australia
Steve Elkington	Australia	Steve Pate	USA
Ernie Els	South Africa	Corey Pavin	USA
Bob Estes	USA	Gary Player	South Africa
Nick Faldo	UK	Nick Price	Zimbabwe
Brad Faxon	USA	Phillip Price	UK
Carlos Franco	Paraguay	Dean Robertson	UK
David Frost	South Africa	Costantino Rocca	Italy
Fred Funk	USA	Justin Rose	UK
Jim Furyk	USA	Raymond Russell	UK
Bill Glasson	USA	Jarmo Sandelin	Sweden
Retief Goosen	South Africa	Vijay Singh	Fiji
Paddy Gribben (A)	UK	Patrik Sjoland	Sweden
Mathias Gronberg	Sweden	Jeff Sluman	USA
Scott Gump	USA	Des Smyth	Ireland
Dudley Hart	USA	Craig Spence	Australia
Tim Herron	USA	Payne Stewart	USA
Scott Hoch	USA	Graeme Storm (A)	UK
David Howell	UK	Steve Stricker	USA
John Huston	USA	Sven Struver	Germany
Tony Jacklin	UK	Hal Sutton	USA
Mark James	UK	Hidemichi Tanaka	Japan
Lee Janzen	USA	Sam Torrance	UK
Miguel Angel Jimenez	Spain	Greg Turner	New Zealand
Brandt Jobe	USA	Bob Tway	USA
Steve Jones	USA	Scott Verplank	USA
Robert Karlsson	Sweden	Tom Watson	USA
Tom Kite	USA	Brian Watts	USA
Choi Kyoung-Ju	Korea	Lee Westwood	UK
Bernhard Langer	Germany	Tiger Woods	USA
Stephen Leaney	Australia	Ian Woosnam	UK

(A) denotes Amateur

Exemption Qualifications

Players who are exempt but have not entered are marked with a §.

Players exempt from Regional and Final Qualifying at time of going to press.

1. First 15 and anyone tying for 15th place in the 1998 Open Championship.

Mark O'Meara	Jesper Parnevik	John Huston
Brian Watts	Davis Love III	Gordon Brand Jnr
Tiger Woods	Costantino Rocca	Jose Maria Olazabal
Raymond Russell	Thomas Bjorn	Peter Baker
Justin Rose	David Duval	Des Smyth
Jim Furyk	Brad Faxon	Greg Turner

2. The Open Champions 1989-1998.

1989–Mark Calcavecchia	1992–Nick Faldo	1997–Justin Leonard
1990–Nick Faldo	1993–Greg Norman	1998–Mark O'Meara
§1991–Ian Baker-Finch	1994–Nick Price	
	1995–John Daly	
	1996–Tom Lehman	

3. Past Open Champions who are under the age of 65 on 18th July 1999 and who are not otherwise exempt.

Gary Player	§Lee Trevino	Severiano Ballesteros
Bob Charles	§Tom Weiskopf	§Bill Rogers
§Jack Nicklaus	Tom Watson	Sandy Lyle
Tony Jacklin	§Johnny Miller	

4. The first 50 players in the Official World Ranking as at 1st June 1999.

David Duval	Fred Couples	Bernhard Langer
Tiger Woods	Hal Sutton	Mark Calcavecchia
Davis Love III	Steve Elkington	Naomichi Ozaki
Ernie Els	Steve Stricker	Glen Day
Colin Montgomerie	Tom Lehman	Bob Tway
Vijay Singh	Lee Janzen	Bob Estes
Mark O'Meara	Brian Watts	Stewart Cink
Lee Westwood	Jose Maria Olazabal	Miguel A Jimenez
Nick Price	Darren Clarke	Andrew Magee
Jim Furyk	Greg Norman	Billy Mayfair
Justin Leonard	Stuart Appleby	Brandt Jobe
Phil Mickelson	Jeff Sluman	Dudley Hart
Payne Stewart	Bill Glasson	Fred Funk
Jeff Maggert	Scott Hoch	Tim Herron
§Jumbo Ozaki	§Loren Roberts	Shigeki Maruyama
Jesper Parnevik	Carlos Franco	Craig Parry
John Huston	Steve Pate	

5. First 20 and anyone tying for 20th place in the Official Money List of the PGA European Tour for 1998.

Colin Montgomerie	Ernie Els	Phillip Price
Darren Clarke	Andrew Coltart	Stephen Allan
Lee Westwood	Mathias Gronberg	Robert Karlsson
Miguel A Jimenez	Stephen Leaney	Bernhard Langer
Patrik Sjoland	Peter Baker	David Carter
Thomas Bjorn	Sven Struver	Ian Woosnam
Jose Maria Olazabal	Sam Torrance	

6. The Volvo PGA Champions for 1996-1999.

1996–Costantino Rocca	1998–Colin Montgomerie
1997–Ian Woosnam	1999–Colin Montgomerie

7. First 5 and anyone tying for 5th place, who are not otherwise exempt, in the top 20 of the Official Money List of the PGA European Tour for 1999 as at 1st June 1999.

Retief Goosen	David Howell	Dean Robertson
Mark James	Jarmo Sandelin	

8. First 5 and anyone tying for 5th place, who are not otherwise exempt, in the top 20 of a cumulative money list taken from all official PGA European Tour events from the Volvo PGA Championship up to and including the Standard Life Loch Lomond. Blank entries will be made on behalf of players qualifying in this category.

9. The US Open Champions for 1990-1999.

§1990–Hale Irwin	1995–Corey Pavin
1991–Payne Stewart	1996–Steve Jones
1992–Tom Kite	1997–Ernie Els
1993–Lee Janzen	1998–Lee Janzen
1994–Ernie Els	1999–Payne Stewart

10. The US Masters Champions for 1995-1999.

1995–Ben Crenshaw	1997–Tiger Woods	1999–Jose Maria Olazabal
1996–Nick Faldo	1998–Mark O'Meara	

David Frost

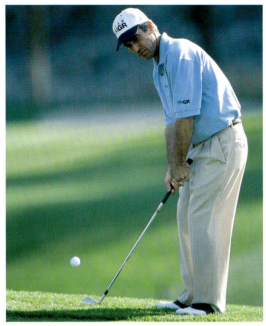

Corey Pavin

11. The USPGA Champions for 1994-1998.

1994–Nick Price 1996–Mark Brooks 1998–Vijay Singh
1995–Steve Elkington 1997–Davis Love III

12. The USPGA Tour Players Champions for 1996-1999.

1996–Fred Couples 1998–Justin Leonard
1997–Steve Elkington 1999–David Duval

13. First 20 and anyone tying for 20th place in the Official Money List of the USPGA Tour for the year ending 31st December 1998.

David Duval	Justin Leonard	Glen Day
Vijay Singh	Fred Couples	Billy Mayfair
Jim Furyk	John Huston	Scott Hoch
Tiger Woods	Davis Love III	Scott Verplank
Hal Sutton	Mark Calcavecchia	Payne Stewart
Phil Mickelson	Steve Stricker	Lee Janzen
Mark O'Meara	Jesper Parnevik	

14. First 5 and anyone tying for 5th place, who are not otherwise exempt, in the top 20 of the Official Points Standing of the USPGA Tour for 1999 as at 1st June 1999.

Scott Gump   Rocco Mediate

15. First 5 and anyone tying for 5th place, who are not otherwise exempt, in the top 20 of a cumulative money list taken from the Players Championship and the five USPGA Tour events leading up to and including the Buick Classic. Blank entries will be made on behalf of players qualifying in this category.

16. Playing members of the 1998 President's Cup teams.

David Duval	Scott Hoch	Steve Elkington
Tiger Woods	Mark Calcavecchia	Stuart Appleby
Jim Furyk	Fred Couples	Carlos Franco
Justin Leonard	John Huston	Shigeki Maruyama
Phil Mickelson	Ernie Els	Craig Parry
Davis Love III	Nick Price	Naomichi Ozaki
Mark O'Meara	Vijay Singh	Frank Nobilo
Hal Sutton	Greg Norman	Greg Turner

17. The Canadian Open Champion for 1998.
Billy Andrade

18. The Japan Open Champion for 1998.
Hidemichi Tanaka

19. The leading player and anyone tying for 1st place on the Asian Golf Tour for 1999.
Choi Kyoung-Ju

20. First 3 and anyone tying for 3rd place on the Australasian Tour for 1998/99.

Jarrod Moseley   Rodney Pampling   Craig Spence

21. First 3 and anyone tying for 3rd place on the Japan Tour for 1998.

§Jumbo Ozaki   Brian Watts   Hidemichi Tanaka

22. First 2 and anyone tying for 2nd place on the Southern Africa Tour for 1998/99.

David Frost   Scott Dunlap

23. First 4 and anyone tying for 4th place, who are not otherwise exempt, in the top 20 of a cumulative money list taken from the Japan PGA Championship and the six Japan PGA Tour events leading up to and including the Mizuno Open. Blank entries will be made on behalf of players qualifying in this category.

24. The leading player, not otherwise exempt, in the 1999 Mizuno Open Championship. Blank entries will be made on behalf of players qualifying in this category.

25. The Senior British Open Champion for 1998.
§Brian Huggett

26. The Amateur Champion for 1999.
Graeme Storm (A)

27. The USA Amateur Champion for 1998.
§Hank Kuehne (A)

28. The European Individual Amateur Champion for 1998.
Paddy Gribben (A)

Note: Exemption for performance as an Amateur under (26) to (28) inclusive will only be granted if the Competitor concerned is still an Amateur on 15th July 1999.

Choi Kyoung-Ju

Some people measure a putter by how many tournaments it has won.

Some people measure a putter by how much money it has won.

Some people measure a putter by how many pros use it.

Measure it however you want.

You still get the same putter.

No other putter comes close to measuring up to Odyssey. It's the success story of the modern game. Every day, more and more tournament professionals are learning how much their game can be enhanced with an Odyssey putter*. It would be no exaggeration to say that our revolutionary Stronomic® technology has changed the face of putting as well as the game of golf itself. So if you want more success on the greens, use the putter that's setting entirely new standards in golf. Visit your local Odyssey Preferred Retailer now.

ODYSSEY®
Number one putter in golf™

* The PGA European Tour is monitored by Sports Marketing Surveys Ltd and the PGA, SPGA, LPGA and Nike Tours by the Darrell Survey Company. Odyssey®, The Number One Putter in Golf™ and Stronomic® are trademarks of Callaway Golf Company.

Past Winners of the Open Championship

Year	Winner	Course	Score
1860	W. Park	Prestwick	174
1861	T. Morris, Sen.	Prestwick	163
1862	T. Morris, Sen.	Prestwick	163
1863	W. Park	Prestwick	168
1864	T. Morris, Sen.	Prestwick	167
1865	A. Strath	Prestwick	162
1866	W. Park	Prestwick	169
1867	T. Morris, Sen.	Prestwick	170
1868	T. Morris, Jun.	Prestwick	157
1869	T. Morris, Jun.	Prestwick	154
1870	T. Morris, Jun.	Prestwick	149

The Belt was won three times in succession by Tom Morris, Jun. and became his property.

Year	Winner	Course	Score
1871	(No Championship)		
1872	T. Morris, Jun.	Prestwick	166
1873	Tom Kidd	St. Andrews	179
1874	Mungo Park	Musselburgh	159
1875	Willie Park	Prestwick	166
1876	Bob Martin	St. Andrews	176
1877	J. Anderson	Musselburgh	160
1878	J. Anderson	Prestwick	157
1879	J. Anderson	St. Andrews	169
1880	B. Ferguson	Musselburgh	162
1881	B. Ferguson	Prestwick	170
1882	B. Ferguson	St. Andrews	171
1883	W. Fernie	Musselburgh	159
1884	J. Simpson	Prestwick	160
1885	Bob Martin	St. Andrews	171
1886	D. Brown	Musselburgh	157
1887	W. Park, Jun.	Prestwick	161
1888	Jack Burns	St. Andrews	171
1889	W. Park, Jun.	Musselburgh	155
1890	Mr. John Ball	Prestwick	164
1891	Hugh Kirkaldy	St. Andrews	166

72 holes played in succeeding years

Year	Winner	Course	Score
1892	Mr. H. H. Hilton	Muirfield	305
1893	W. Auchterlonie	Prestwick	322
1894	J. H. Taylor	Sandwich	326
1895	J. H. Taylor	St. Andrews	322
1896	H. Vardon	Muirfield	316
1897	Mr. H. H. Hilton	Hoylake	314
1898	H. Vardon	Prestwick	307
1899	H. Vardon	Sandwich	310
1900	J. H. Taylor	St. Andrews	309
1901	James Braid	Muirfield	309
1902	Alex Herd	Hoylake	307
1903	H. Vardon	Prestwick	300
1904	Jack White	Sandwich	296
1905	James Braid	St. Andrews	318
1906	James Braid	Muirfield	300
1907	A. Massy	Hoylake	312
1908	James Braid	Prestwick	291
1909	J. H. Taylor	Deal	295
1910	James Braid	St. Andrews	299
1911	H. Vardon	Sandwich	303
1912	E. Ray	Muirfield	295
1913	J. H. Taylor	Hoylake	304
1914	H. Vardon	Prestwick	306
1915-19	(No Championship)		
1920	G. Duncan	Deal	303
1921	J. Hutchison	St. Andrews	296
1922	W. Hagen	Sandwich	300
1923	A. G. Havers	Troon	295
1924	W. Hagen	Hoylake	301
1925	J. Barnes	Prestwick	300
1926	Mr. R. T. Jones	R. Lytham	291
1927	Mr. R. T. Jones	St. Andrews	285
1928	W. Hagen	Sandwich	292
1929	W. Hagen	Muirfield	292
1930	Mr. R. T. Jones	Hoylake	291
1931	T. D. Armour	Carnoustie	296
1932	G. Sarazen	Princes	283
1933	D. Shute	St. Andrews	292
1934	T. H. Cotton	Sandwich	283
1935	A. Perry	Muirfield	283
1936	A. H. Padgham	Hoylake	287
1937	T. H. Cotton	Carnoustie	290
1938	R. A. Whitcombe	Sandwich	295
1939	R. Burton	St. Andrews	290
1940-45	(No Championship)		
1946	S. Snead	St. Andrews	290
1947	F. Daly	Hoylake	293
1948	T. H. Cotton	Muirfield	284
1949	A. D. Locke	Sandwich	283
1950	A. D. Locke	Troon	279
1951	M. Faulkner	R. Portrush	285
1952	A. D. Locke	R. Lytham	287
1953	B. Hogan	Carnoustie	282
1954	P. W. Thomson	R. Birkdale	283
1955	P. W. Thomson	St. Andrews	281
1956	P. W. Thomson	Hoylake	286
1957	A. D. Locke	St. Andrews	279
1958	P. W. Thomson	R. Lytham	278
1959	G. J. Player	Muirfield	284
1960	K. D. G. Nagle	St. Andrews	278
1961	A. Palmer	R. Birkdale	284
1962	A. Palmer	Troon	276
1963	R. Charles	R. Lytham	277
1964	A. D. Lema	St. Andrews	279
1965	P. W. Thomson	R. Birkdale	285
1966	J. Nicklaus	Muirfield	282
1967	R. de Vicenzo	Hoylake	278
1968	G. J. Player	Carnoustie	289
1969	A. Jacklin	R. Lytham	280
1970	J. Nicklaus	St. Andrews	283
1971	L. Trevino	R. Birkdale	278
1972	L. Trevino	Muirfield	278
1973	T. Weiskopf	Troon	276
1974	G. Player	R. Lytham	282
1975	T. Watson	Carnoustie	279
1976	J. Miller	R. Birkdale	279
1977	T. Watson	Turnberry	268
1978	J. Nicklaus	St. Andrews	281
1979	S. Ballesteros	R. Lytham	283
1980	T. Watson	Muirfield	271
1981	B. Rogers	Sandwich	276
1982	T. Watson	R. Troon	284
1983	T. Watson	R. Birkdale	275
1984	S. Ballesteros	St. Andrews	276
1985	A. W. B. Lyle	Sandwich	282
1986	G. Norman	Turnberry	280
1987	N. Faldo	Muirfield	279
1988	S. Ballesteros	R. Lytham	273
1989	M. Calcavecchia	R. Troon	275
1990	N. Faldo	St. Andrews	270
1991	I. Baker-Finch	R. Birkdale	272
1992	N. Faldo	Muirfield	272
1993	G. Norman	Sandwich	267
1994	N. Price	Turnberry	268
1995	J. Daly	St. Andrews	282
1996	T. Lehman	R. Lytham	271
1997	J. Leonard	R. Troon	272

Final Score Open Championship at Royal Birkdale 1998

	Name	Country	Score					
1	MARK O'MEARA	U.S.A.	72	68	72	68	–	280
2	BRIAN WATTS	U.S.A.	68	69	73	70	–	280
3	TIGER WOODS	U.S.A.	65	73	77	66	–	281
4	RAYMOND RUSSELL	U.K.	68	73	75	66	–	282
=	JUSTIN ROSE (A)	U.K.	72	66	75	69	–	282
=	JIM FURYK	U.S.A.	70	70	72	70	–	282
=	JESPER PARNEVIK	SWEDEN	68	72	72	70	–	282
8	DAVIS LOVE III	U.S.A.	67	73	77	68	–	285
9	COSTANTINO ROCCA	ITALY	72	74	70	70	–	286
=	THOMAS BJORN	DENMARK	68	71	76	71	–	286
11	DAVID DUVAL	U.S.A.	70	71	75	71	–	287
=	BRAD FAXON	U.S.A.	67	74	74	72	–	287
=	JOHN HUSTON	U.S.A.	65	77	73	72	–	287
14	GORDON BRAND JNR	U.K.	71	70	76	71	–	288
15	JOSE MARIA OLAZABAL	SPAIN	73	72	75	69	–	289
=	PETER BAKER	U.K.	69	72	77	71	–	289
=	DES SMYTH	IRELAND	74	69	75	71	–	289
=	GREG TURNER	NEW ZEALAND	68	75	75	71	–	289
19	ROBERT ALLENBY	AUSTRALIA	67	76	78	69	–	290
=	CURTIS STRANGE	U.S.A.	73	73	74	70	–	290
=	VIJAY SINGH	FIJI	67	74	78	71	–	290
=	MARK JAMES	U.K.	71	74	74	71	–	290
=	SANDY LYLE	U.K.	71	72	75	72	–	290
24	LEE JANZEN	U.S.A.	72	69	80	70	–	291
=	SAM TORRANCE	U.K.	69	77	75	70	–	291
=	PETER O'MALLEY	AUSTRALIA	71	71	78	71	–	291
=	STEPHEN AMES	TRINIDAD & TOBAGO	68	72	79	72	–	291
=	BOB ESTES	U.S.A.	72	70	76	73	–	291
29	SCOTT DUNLAP	U.S.A.	72	69	80	71	–	292
=	NICK PRICE	ZIMBABWE	66	72	82	72	–	292
=	SERGIO GARCIA (A)	SPAIN	69	75	76	72	–	292
=	ERNIE ELS	SOUTH AFRICA	72	74	74	72	–	292
=	LOREN ROBERTS	U.S.A.	66	76	76	74	–	292
=	SHIGEKI MARUYAMA	JAPAN	70	73	75	74	–	292
35	SVEN STRUVER	GERMANY	75	70	80	68	–	293
=	SANTIAGO LUNA	SPAIN	70	72	80	71	–	293
=	MARK CALCAVECCHIA	U.S.A.	69	77	73	74	–	293
38	JOAKIM HAEGGMAN	SWEDEN	71	74	78	71	–	294
=	STEEN TINNING	DENMARK	69	76	77	72	–	294
=	PATRIK SJOLAND	SWEDEN	72	72	77	73	–	294
=	NAOMICHI OZAKI	JAPAN	72	73	76	73	–	294

the 1998
ionship
kdale

Pos	Name	Country	Score					
=	TOM KITE	U.S.A.	72	69	79	74	-	294
=	PHILIP WALTON	IRELAND	68	76	74	76	-	294
44	DAVID HOWELL	U.K.	68	77	79	71	-	295
=	RODGER DAVIS	AUSTRALIA	76	70	78	71	-	295
=	DAVID FROST	SOUTH AFRICA	72	73	78	72	-	295
=	DAVID CARTER	U.K.	71	75	76	73	-	295
=	PAYNE STEWART	U.S.A.	71	71	78	75	-	295
=	NICK FALDO	U.K.	72	73	75	75	-	295
=	ANDREW COLTART	U.K.	68	77	75	75	-	295
=	KATSUYOSHI TOMORI	JAPAN	75	71	70	79	-	295
52	BRANDT JOBE	U.S.A.	70	73	82	71	-	296
=	LARRY MIZE	U.S.A.	70	75	79	72	-	296
=	STEVE STRICKER	U.S.A.	70	72	80	74	-	296
=	BILLY MAYFAIR	U.S.A.	72	73	77	74	-	296
=	FRANKIE MINOZA	PHILIPPINES	69	75	76	76	-	296
57	JUSTIN LEONARD	U.S.A.	73	73	82	69	-	297
=	TREVOR DODDS	NAMIBIA	73	71	81	72	-	297
=	IGNACIO GARRIDO	SPAIN	71	74	80	72	-	297
=	STEVE JONES	U.S.A.	73	72	79	73	-	297
=	GREG CHALMERS	AUSTRALIA	71	75	77	74	-	297
=	IAN WOOSNAM	U.K.	72	74	76	75	-	297
=	EDUARDO ROMERO	ARGENTINA	71	70	79	77	-	297
64	LEE WESTWOOD	U.K.	71	71	78	78	-	298
=	CARLOS FRANCO	PARAGUAY	71	73	76	78	-	298
66	STEWART CINK	U.S.A.	71	73	83	72	-	299
=	MICHAEL CAMPBELL	NEW ZEALAND	73	73	80	73	-	299
=	DIDIER DE VOOGHT (A)	BELGIUM	70	76	80	73	-	299
=	MICHAEL LONG	NEW ZEALAND	70	74	78	77	-	299
=	MARK BROOKS	U.S.A.	71	73	75	80	-	299
=	FRED COUPLES	U.S.A.	66	74	78	81	-	299
72	ANDREW CLAPP	U.K.	72	74	81	73	-	300
73	GARY EVANS	U.K.	69	74	84	74	-	301
74	BOB MAY	U.S.A.	70	73	85	75	-	303
75	ANDREW McLARDY	SOUTH AFRICA	72	74	80	78	-	304
76	FREDRIK JACOBSON	SWEDEN	67	78	81	79	-	305
77	KAZUHIKO HOSOKAWA	JAPAN	72	73	81	80	-	306
78	ROBERT GILES	U.K.	72	74	83	78	-	307
79	PHIL MICKELSON	U.S.A.	71	74	85	78	-	308
80	ANDREW OLDCORN	U.K.	75	71	84	79	-	309
81	DUDLEY HART	U.S.A.	73	72	85	80	-	310

Our Famous Links.

Darren Clarke

While the Portmarnock Hotel and Golf Links is set in splendid surroundings, the house was originally owned by the Jameson family, famous for their Irish Whiskey. Their home has been tastefully converted

to an international four star hotel with the grounds now hosting a magnificent 18 hole golf links.

Not surprisingly it has received a number of prestigious awards from the AA and RAC including the Black & White Hotel Bar of the Year, 1997.

Darren Clarke, Ireland's number one golfer and the Irish representative on last Sept-ember's winning European Ryder Cup team represents Portmarnock Hotel & Golf Links as Touring Professional on the world's golfing stage. The Links course was designed by fellow Ryder Cup player Bernhard

Langer and has gained widespread recognition among the golfing fraternity as one of the premier links courses in the country. Offering both professional and amateur golfer all the traditions of an original links course, along with the challenge of the modern game. Remember the course is open all year round... to everyone.

Portmarnock Hotel and Golf Links

Portmarnock, Co. Dublin, Ireland.
Phone for a reservation: ++353 1 846 0511. Fax: ++353 1 846 2442 http://www.portmarnock.com

Where nothing is overlooked... but the sea

Sandy Lyle

GREAT BRITAIN

BORN
9TH FEBRUARY 1958, SHREWSBURY, ENGLAND

MAJORS
THE OPEN 1985 • US MASTERS 1988

The 128th Open Golf Championship Carnoustie

Red Route	———
Spectator stands	■
Toilets	T
Catering	C
First aid	+
Crossing points	(3a)—(3a)

THE RED ROUTE
The 'Red Route' is for the benefit of spectators who may wish to follow a particular game.

- ADMISSION BADGES MUST BE WORN AT ALL TIMES
- NO DOGS OR STEPLADDERS
- NO CAMERAS ON CHAMPIONSHIP DAYS

Card of the Course

Hole	Yards	Par	Hole	Yards	Par
1	407	4	10	466	4
2	462	4	11	383	4
3	342	4	12	479	4
4	412	4	13	169	3
5	411	4	14	515	5
6	578	5	15	472	4
7	412	4	16	250	3
8	183	3	17	459	4
9	474	4	18	487	4
OUT	3681	36	IN	3680	35
			OUT	3681	36
			TOTAL	7361	71

Open Champ

MOST VICTORIES
6. Harry Vardon, 1896-98-99-1903-11-14
5. James Braid, 1901-05-06-08-10; J. H. Taylor, 1894-95-1900-09-13; Peter Thomson, 1954-55-56-58-65; Tom Watson, 1975-77-80-82-83

MOST TIMES RUNNER-UP OR JOINT RUNNER-UP
7. Jack Nicklaus, 1964-67-68-72-76-77-79
6. J. H. Taylor, 1896-1904-05-06-07-14

OLDEST WINNER
Old Tom Morris. 46 years 99 days, 1867
Roberto de Vicenzo. 44 years 93 days, 1967

YOUNGEST WINNER
Young Tom Morris. 17 years 5 months 8 days, 1868
Willie Auchterlonie. 21 years 24 days, 1893
Severiano Ballesteros. 22 years 3 months 12 days, 1979

YOUNGEST AND OLDEST COMPETITOR
Young Tom Morris. 14 years, 4 months, 4 days, 1865
Gene Sarazen. 71 years 4 months 13 days, 1973

BIGGEST MARGIN OF VICTORY
13 strokes. Old Tom Morris, 1862
12 strokes. Young Tom Morris, 1870
8 strokes. J. H. Taylor, 1900 and 1913; James Braid, 1908
6 strokes. Bobby Jones, 1927; Walter Hagen, 1929; Arnold Palmer. 1962; Johnny Miller, 1976

LOWEST WINNING AGGREGATES
267 (66, 68, 69, 64) Greg Norman, Royal St George's, 1993
268 (68, 70, 65, 65) Tom Watson, Turnberry, 1977
   (69, 66, 67, 66) Nick Price, Turnberry, 1994
270 (67, 65, 67, 71) Nick Faldo, St Andrews, 1990
271 (68, 70, 64, 69) Tom Watson, Muirfield, 1980
   (67, 67, 64, 73) Tom Lehman, Royal Lytham & St. Annes 1996
272 (71, 71, 64, 66) Ian Baker-Finch, Royal Birkdale, 1991
   (66, 64, 69, 73) Nick Faldo, Muirfield, 1992
   (69, 66, 72, 65) Justin Leonard, Royal Troon, 1997

LOWEST AGGREGATES BY RUNNER-UP
269 (68, 70, 65, 66) Jack Nicklaus, Turnberry, 1977
   (69, 63, 70, 67) Nick Faldo, Royal St George's, 1993
   (68, 66, 68, 67) Jesper Parnevik, Turnberry, 1994
273 (66, 67, 70, 70) John Cook, Muirfield, 1992
   (67, 69, 71, 66) Mark McCumber, Royal Lytham & St. Annes, 1996
   (68, 67, 71, 67) Ernie Els, Royal Lytham & St. Annes, 1996

LOWEST AGGREGATE BY AN AMATEUR
281 (68, 72, 70, 71) Iain Pyman, Royal St George's, 1993
   (75, 66, 70, 70), Tiger Woods, Royal Lytham & St. Annes, 1996
282 (72, 66, 75, 69), Justin Rose, Royal Birkdale, 1998
283 (74, 70, 71, 68) Guy Wolstenholme, St Andrews, 1960

LOWEST INDIVIDUAL ROUND
63. Mark Hayes, second round, Turnberry, 1977; Isao Aoki, third round, Muirfield, 1980; Greg Norman, second round, Turnberry, 1986; Paul Broadhurst, third round, St Andrews, 1990; Jodie Mudd, fourth round, Royal Birkdale, 1991; Nick Faldo, second round, and Payne Stewart, fourth round, Royal St George's, 1993

LOWEST INDIVIDUAL ROUND BY AN AMATEUR
66. Frank Stranahan, fourth round, Troon, 1950
66. Tiger Woods, second round, Royal Lytham & St. Annes, 1996
66. Justin Rose, second round, Royal Birkdale, 1998

LOWEST FIRST ROUND
64. Craig Stadler, Royal Birkdale, 1983; Christy O'Connor Jr., Royal St George's, 1985; Rodger Davis, Muirfield, 1987; Raymond Floyd and Steve Pate, Muirfield, 1992

LOWEST SECOND ROUND
63. Mark Hayes, Turnberry, 1977; Greg Norman, Turnberry, 1986; Nick Faldo, Royal St George's, 1993

LOWEST THIRD ROUND
63. Isao Aoki, Muirfield, 1980; Paul Broadhurst, St Andrews, 1990

LOWEST FOURTH ROUND
63. Jodie Mudd, Royal Birkdale, 1991; Payne Stewart, Royal St George's, 1993

LOWEST FIRST 36 HOLES
130 (66, 64) Nick Faldo, Muirfield, 1992
132 (67, 65) Henry Cotton, Sandwich, 1934;
   (66, 66) Greg Norman and (67, 65) Nick Faldo, St Andrews, 1990;
   (69, 63), Nick Faldo, Royal St George's, 1993

LOWEST SECOND 36 HOLES
130 (65, 65) Tom Watson, Turnberry, 1977;
   (64, 66) Ian Baker-Finch, Royal Birkdale, 1991;
   (66, 64) Anders Forsbrand, Turnberry, 1994

LOWEST FIRST 54 HOLES
198 (67, 67, 64) Tom Lehman, Royal Lytham & St. Annes 1996
199 (67, 65, 67) Nick Faldo, St Andrews, 1990;
   (66, 64, 69), Nick Faldo, Muirfield, 1992

LOWEST FINAL 54 HOLES
199 (66, 67, 66) Nick Price, Turnberry, 1994
200 (70, 65, 65) Tom Watson, Turnberry, 1977;
   (63, 70, 67) Nick Faldo, Royal St George's, 1993;
   (66, 70, 64) Nick Faldo and (66, 64, 70), Fuzzy Zoeller, Turnberry, 1994

LOWEST 9 HOLES
28. Denis Durnian, first 9, Royal Birkdale, 1983
29. Peter Thomson and Tom Haliburton, first 9 Royal Lytham, 1958; Tony Jacklin, first 9, St Andrews, 1970; Bill Longmuir, first 9, Royal Lytham, 1979; David J. Russell, first 9, Royal Lytham, 1988; Ian Baker-Finch and Paul Broadhurst, first 9, St Andrews, 1990; Ian Baker-Finch, first 9, Royal Birkdale, 1991; Paul McGinley, first 9, Royal Lytham & St. Annes 1996

CHAMPIONS IN THREE DECADES
Harry Vardon 1896, 1903, 1911
J. H. Taylor 1894, 1900, 1913
Gary Player 1959, 1968, 1974

BIGGEST SPAN BETWEEN FIRST AND LAST VICTORIES
19 years. J. H. Taylor, 1894-1913
18 years. Harry Vardon, 1896-1914
15 years. Gary Player, 1959-74
14 years. Henry Cotton, 1934-48

SUCCESSIVE VICTORIES
4. Young Tom Morris, 1868-72. No championship in 1871
3. Jamie Anderson, 1877-79; Bob Ferguson, 1880-82; Peter Thomson, 1954-56
2. Old Tom Morris, 1861-62; J. H. Taylor, 1894-95; Harry Vardon, 1898-99; James Braid, 1905-06; Bobby Jones, 1926-27; Walter Hagen, 1928-29; Bobby Locke, 1949-50; Arnold Palmer, 1961-62; Lee Trevino, 1971-72; Tom Watson, 1982-83

VICTORIES BY AMATEURS
3. Bobby Jones, 1926-27-30
2. Harold Hilton, 1892-97
1. John Ball, 1890
Roger Wethered lost a play-off in 1921

HIGHEST NUMBER OF TOP FIVE FINISHES
16. J. J. H. Taylor, Jack Nicklaus
15. Harry Vardon, James Braid

Championship Statistics

HIGHEST NUMBER OF ROUNDS UNDER 70
33. Jack Nicklaus; Nick Faldo
27. Tom Watson
23. Greg Norman
21. Lee Trevino
20. Severiano Ballesteros; Nick Price

FIRST PLAYERS TO BREAK 70 IN THE OPEN
68. J H Taylor (4)
69. James Braid (3); Jack White (4)
1904 Royal St. George's

OUTRIGHT LEADER AFTER EVERY ROUND
Willie Auchterlonie, 1893; J. H. Taylor, 1894 and 1900; James Braid, 1908; Ted Ray, 1912; Bobby Jones, 1927; Gene Sarazen, 1932; Henry Cotton, 1934; Tom Weiskopf, 1973;

RECORD LEADS (SINCE 1892)
After 18 holes:
4 strokes, James Braid, 1908; Bobby Jones, 1927;
Henry Cotton, 1934;
Christy O'Connor Jr., 1985
After 36 holes:
9 strokes, Henry Cotton, 1934
After 54 holes:
10 strokes, Henry Cotton, 1934;
7 strokes, Tony Lema, 1964;
6 strokes, James Braid, 1908, Tom Lehman, 1996

CHAMPIONS WITH EACH ROUND LOWER THAN PREVIOUS ONE
Jack White. 1904, Sandwich, 80, 75, 72, 69
James Braid. 1906, Muirfield, 77, 76, 74, 73
Ben Hogan. 1953, Carnoustie, 73, 71, 70, 68
Gary Player. 1959, Muirfield, 75, 71, 70, 68

CHAMPION WITH FOUR ROUNDS THE SAME
Densmore Shute. 1933, St Andrews, 73, 73, 73, 73
(excluding the play-off)

BIGGEST VARIATION BETWEEN ROUNDS OF A CHAMPION
14 strokes. Henry Cotton, 1934, second round 65, fourth round, 79
11 strokes. Jack White, 1904, first round 80, fourth round 69;
Greg Norman, 1986, first round 74, second round 63, third round 74

BIGGEST VARIATION BETWEEN TWO ROUNDS
18 strokes. A. Tingey Jnr, 1923, First Round 94, second round 76
17 strokes. Jack Nicklaus, 1981, first round 83, second round 66
17 strokes. Ian Baker-Finch, 1986, first round 86, second round 69

BEST COMEBACK BY CHAMPIONS
After 18 holes:
Harry Vardon, 1896, 11 strokes behind the leader
After 36 holes:
George Duncan, 1920, 13 strokes behind the leader
After 54 holes:
Jim Barnes, 1925, 5 strokes behind the leader;
Tommy Armour, 1931, 5 strokes behind the leader;
Justin Leonard, 1997, 5 strokes behind the leader
Of non-Champions, Greg Norman, 1989, 7 strokes behind the leader and lost in a play-off

CHAMPIONS WITH FOUR ROUNDS UNDER 70
Greg Norman. 1993, Royal St George's, 66, 68, 69, 64
Nick Price. 1994, Turnberry, 69, 66, 67, 66
Of non-Champions. Ernie Els, 1993, Royal St George's, 68, 69, 69, 68;
Jesper Parnevik. 1994, Turnberry, 68, 66, 68, 67

BEST FINISHING ROUND BY A CHAMPION
64. Greg Norman, Royal St George's, 1993
65. Tom Watson, Turnberry, 1977; Severiano Ballesteros, Royal Lytham, 1988; Justin Leonard, Royal Troon, 1997;
66. Johnny Miller, Royal Birkdale, 1976; Ian Baker-Finch, Royal Birkdale, 1991; Nick Price, Turnberry, 1994

WORST FINISHING ROUND BY A CHAMPION SINCE 1920
79. Henry Cotton, Sandwich, 1934
78. Reg Whitcombe, Sandwich, 1938
77. Walter Hagen, Hoylake, 1924

WORST OPENING ROUND BY A CHAMPION SINCE 1919
80. George Duncan, Deal, 1920 (he also had a second round of 80)
77. Walter Hagen, Hoylake, 1924

BEST OPENING ROUND BY A CHAMPION
66. Peter Thomson, Royal Lytham, 1958; Nick Faldo, Muirfield 1992; Greg Norman, Royal St George's, 1993
67. Henry Cotton, Sandwich, 1934; Tom Watson, Royal Birkdale, 1983; Severiano Ballesteros, Royal Lytham, 1988; Nick Faldo, St Andrews, 1990; John Daly, St Andrews 1995; Tom Lehman, Royal Lytham & St. Annes, 1996

BIGGEST RECOVERY IN 18 HOLES BY A CHAMPION
George Duncan, Deal. 1920, was 13 strokes behind the leader, Abe Mitchell. After 36 holes and level after 54

MOST APPEARANCES ON FINAL DAY (SINCE 1892)
32. Jack Nicklaus
30. J. H. Taylor
27. Harry Vardon, James Braid
26. Peter Thomson, Gary Player
23. Dai Rees
22. Henry Cotton

CHAMPIONSHIP WITH HIGHEST NUMBER OF ROUNDS UNDER 70
148. Turnberry, 1994
116. Royal St George's, 1993
102. Royal Birkdale, 1991

CHAMPIONSHIP SINCE 1946 WITH THE FEWEST ROUNDS UNDER 70
St Andrews. 1946; Hoylake. 1947; Portrush. 1951; Hoylake, 1956; Carnoustie. 1968. All had only two rounds under 70

COURSES MOST OFTEN USED
St Andrews, 25; Prestwick, 24; Muirfield, 14; Sandwich, 12; Hoylake, 10; Royal Lytham, 9; Royal Birkdale, 8; Royal Troon, 7; Musselburgh, 6; Carnoustie, 5; Turnberry, 3; Deal, 2; Royal Portrush and Prince's, 1

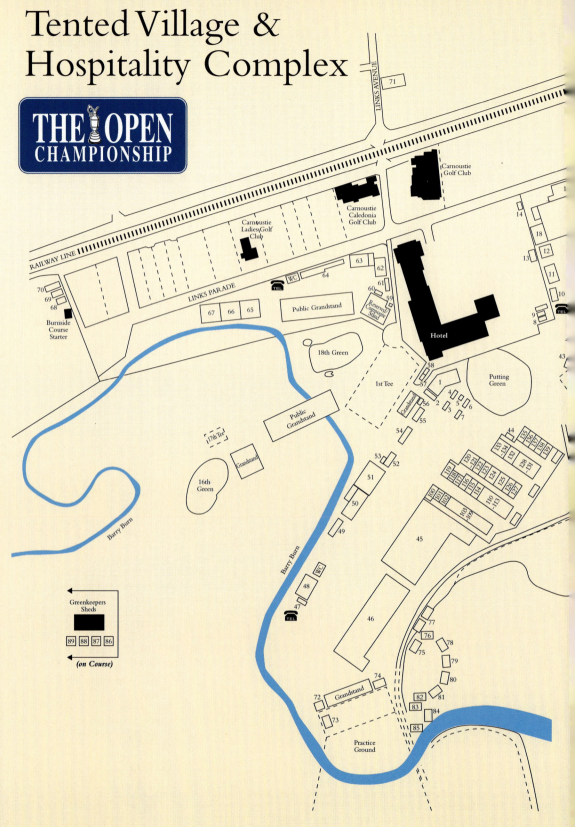

Angus & Dundee Tourist Board	22
Bollinger Tent	25
British Aerospace plc	65
Building Control & Environmental Health	30
Caddie Master (HQ)	68
Caddie Rest Room 1	69
Caddie Rest Room 2	70
Carnoustie Championship Committee	61
Carnoustie Country	51
Charity – Children 1st	41
Chief Marshal HQ	3
Competitors Family Marquee	63
Competitors Physiotherapy Unit	64
Courtaulds Textiles	66
Courtesy Car HQ	14
Diamond Vision Screen	19
ESPN	6
European Golf Industry Association	40
Famous Grouse – 19th Hole	50
Fire Prevention	21
First Aid	42
Golf Club Stewards Association	29
British & International Golf Greenkeepers Association	11
Greenkeepers Equipment	57
Greenkeepers HQ	58
Greenways Marketing Office	37
Group 4 Security HQ	9
Halcrow Crouch – Consulting Engineers	10
Home Unions	27
Hospitality Reception	44
Imaging Tent	16
Information Centre	52
Information Centre Rest Cabin	53
Job Centre	32
Left Luggage	28/34/47
Litter Control	71
Lost Property (Tayside Police)	20
Main Scoreboard	54
Medical HQ	64
Night Sheet Store	39
Nikon – Binocular Hire	55
Official Merchandise	43/49
Open Golf Show	38
Pearce Maintenance – Rolex	8
PGA European Tour	60
Press Centre	15
Press Interview Cabin	17
Press Interview Tent	18
Professional Golfers Association	24
Professionals Shop	35
Programme Publications Ltd	4
Public Catering	23/46
R&A Championship Committee	62
R&A Championship Offices	1
R&A Club Tent & Composite Ticket Holders	45
Radio Interview Cabin	59
Registry/Recorders	2
Royal Bank of Scotland plc	48
Schweppes Europe	67
Schweppes Junior Golf Tent	36
Score Control	13
Scoreboard Cabin	56
Scoreboard Carriers HQ	5
Scorers HQ	7
Seafood Restaurant	26
Site Reporting Office	33
Staff Office	31
Unisys	12

PRACTICE GROUND

Apollo Sports Technologies	73
Callaway Golf Pro Tour Service Centre	79
Golfee Products	74
Maxfli Golf	82
Mizuno Mobile Workshop	81
Nikon – Camera Loan	72
PGA European Tour Field Vehicles	77
Ping Golf Equipment	76
Spalding Sports UK Ltd	78
Taylor Made Tour Support Vehicle	80
Titleist & Foot-Joy Worldwide	83-85
Wilson Tour Vehicle	75

HOSPITALITY COMPLEX

Payne & Gunter	100-139
Town & County	150-213

GREENKEEPERS SHEDS

Chief Marshal Reporting Office	88
First Aid	89
Group 4 Night Security HQ	87
R&A I&B Office	86

When it comes to sports results, you could say we really know the score.

In sports - just like business - results are everything. And not just to the millions worldwide who depend on our systems to deliver real-time scores and analysis of premier sporting events on the Web and on TV - but to the networks and press that cover them. Events like the PGA European Tour, The Open Championship, U.S. Open, U.S. Seniors Open, U.S. Women's Open, Australian Open, Rugby World Cup, Macau Grand Prix and many more. We ensure the results keep pouring in thanks to the powerful teaming of Unisys software, Windows NT servers and our dedicated people. It's the same combination our customers around the world rely on to solve their real-time business problems and get them results. Which is why we take sports very seriously - it's what keeps us ahead of the game. www.unisys.com.

©1999 Unisys Corporation.

UNISYS We eat, sleep and drink this stuff.

Ian Woosnam

GREAT BRITAIN

BORN
2ND MARCH 1958, OSWESTRY, WALES

MAJORS
US MASTERS 1991

The Open Golf Show

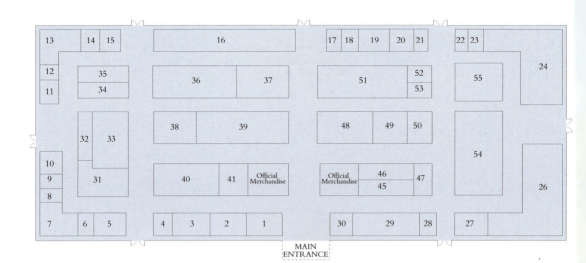

J.A. Tonge Ltd International Main Office 30	Maxfli/Reebok Golf 36
Alfred Dunhill Ltd 40	Millers 8
Andalucia Golf 20	Myrtle Beach Golf Holiday 12
Ashworth UK Ltd 7	Nike Golf 26
Baxter Prints 1	North Carolina Golf 53
Bobby Jones 10	Northern Ireland Tourist Board 17
Burberry Golf 31	Old Troon Sporting Antiques 5
Canon European Masters 9	Osan Ltd 15
Caledonian Golf Group 46	Peter Scott Knitwear 11
Callaway Golf – Odyssey 54	Ping Golf Equipment 39
Carnoustie Country 4	Portugal 13
Ceres Sports Ltd 2	Pringle of Scotland 16
Coastal South Carolina, USA 52	Rhod McEwan Golf Books 41
Cotswold Golf Shoes 50	Scotland – Home of Golf 23
Elmwood College, Fife, Scotland 22	Slazenger Golf 37
Fade Clothing 47	Spain Golf 19
Golf in France 14	Spalding Sports 35
Greg Norman Collection UK 38	St Andrews Links Trust 32
Hamilton & Inches, Edinburgh (Jewellers) 45	Strang The Jewellers 3
Hill Billy Powered Golf Trolley 55	Stylo Golf 29
Hugo Boss 33	Taylor Made Golf 51
Irish Tourist Board 18	The Royal Bank of Scotland Classic and Gold MasterCards 28
Lacoste 27	Tirion Seat Sticks 21
Lyle & Scott 24	Titleist and Foot-Joy Worldwide 48
Lynx 49	Tunisia 6
	Wilson Sporting Goods 34

The Open Golf Show is open 9.00am—6.30pm Monday 12th–

Saturday 17th July, and 9.00am—5.00pm Sunday 18th July

the ultimate golfing shopping experience..

GOLF EXHIBITION

The National Golf Show
golf live '99

Try out and buy the latest in equipment & apparel •
Meet top pros and golf celebrities •
Get advice from the top instructors •

- Pitching & Putting Greens
- Driving Bays
- Electronic 3D Simulators & Analysers
- Fashion Shows
- Holidays & Resorts Feature Area
- Junior Coaching Feature Area
- Virtual Zone
- Free prize draws and Competitions
  to win equipment, apparel, tickets to tournaments and a fabulous golf vacation
- Free admission to under 16's
- Interactive Fun for all the family!
- Live coverage of the Dutch Open
- Refreshments available all day

Official Charity

NSPCC
Cruelty to children must stop. FULL STOP.

Reg. Charity No. 216401

...don't miss the golfing extravaganza of the year

ticket hotline 0870 739 9777

Tickets available in advance £8.00 • On the day £12.00 • Under 16's No charge

National Rate - approx. 10p per minute   (Under 16's must be accompanied by an adult & Identity may be required)   www.golflive.co.uk

London • Wembley Exhibition Centre • 23rd-25th July 1999
10.00am - 7.00pm Friday & Saturday • 10.00am - 6.00pm Sunday

Jim Furyk

UNITED STATES

BORN
12TH MAY 1970, WEST CHESTER, PENNSYLVANIA

"When you're at the world's most prestigious golf championship, why not join me at one of the world's most prestigious hotels?"

The Millennium Open Golf Championship
St. Andrews, Scotland
18-25 July 2000

Tony Jacklin OBE
Open Champion 1969

WHERE will you stay during the Millennium Open Championship? QE2 – the world's most famous liner – will sail overnight from Southampton, England, to Scotland's home of golf, the internationally renowned Old Course at St. Andrews.

Meet and listen to Tony Jacklin OBE, on board the QE2.

During this unique millennium seven night event, the QE2 will provide luxury floating hotel accommodation for the duration of the Open Golf Championship.

Your package will include luxury accommodation, all meals on board the QE2, daily course admission to the Open Golf Championship, shore transfer, evening entertainment every night and much more.

This unique golf cruise, represents a highly attractive exclusive opportunity for conference, corporate and leisure travel. *Prices from US Dollar $2,999 per person.*

SCOTIA GOLF 2000 LTD
57 Bothwell Street, Glasgow G2 6RF, Scotland, U.K.
TEL: 0141 305 5050 FAX: 0141 305 5051
email: bill@scotiatravel.com   www.scotiatravel.com

 # Future Venues

2000
THE OLD COURSE, ST ANDREWS
20TH–23RD JULY

2001

ROYAL LYTHAM & ST ANNES

19TH–22ND JULY

2002

MUIRFIELD

18TH–21ST JULY

Official Suppliers

The Championship Committee of the Royal & Ancient Golf Club acknowledges the assistance of the following suppliers

Nikon

UNISYS

1999 OPEN GOLF CHAMPIONSHIP PROGRAMME

Programme produced by
Programme Publications Group Ltd., Bradford House, 39A East Street, Epsom, Surrey KT17 1BL
Tel: 01372 743377 **email:** lynn@programmepubs.demon.co.uk **website:** www.eventprogrammes.com

Design and Artwork by
Creative Services Ltd., 20 Tower Street, Brunswick Business Park, Liverpool L3 4BJ **Tel:** 0151 707 4200

Reprographics by Speedgraphics **Tel:** 0151 336 6299

Printed by Inglis Allen **Tel:** 01592 267201

Photography by
Allsport, Popperfoto, Eric Hepworth, Alex Jackson, DC Thomson, Michael Joy, Mark Newcombe

No parts of this programme may be reproduced without permission in writing from
The Royal & Ancient Golf Club of St Andrews.